GW00739032

...experience and a passion for travel.

**Rely on Thomas Cook as your travelling companion on your next trip and benefit from our unique heritage.**

Thomas Cook **pocket** guides

# CRETE

Your travelling companion since 1873

Written by Brian and Eileen Anderson, updated by Carole French

**Published by Thomas Cook Publishing**
A division of Thomas Cook Tour Operations Limited
Company registration no. 3772199 England
The Thomas Cook Business Park, Unit 9, Coningsby Road,
Peterborough PE3 8SB, United Kingdom
Email: books@thomascook.com, Tel: +44 (0) 1733 416477
www.thomascookpublishing.com

**Produced by Cambridge Publishing Management Limited**
Burr Elm Court, Main Street, Caldecote CB23 7NU
www.cambridgepm.co.uk

ISBN: 978-1-84848-384-2

© 2006, 2008 Thomas Cook Publishing
This third edition © 2011
Text © Thomas Cook Publishing
Maps © Thomas Cook Publishing/PCGraphics (UK) Limited

Series Editor: Karen Beaulah
Production/DTP: Steven Collins

Printed and bound in Spain by GraphyCems

Cover photography © Hemis.fr/SuperStock

# CONTENTS

**INTRODUCTION** ............5
Getting to know Crete .................8
The best of Crete.........................10
Symbols key.................................12

**RESORTS** .....................13
Chania.........................................14
Paleochora...................................20
Aghia Marina &
    Platanias................................22
Rethymnon..................................27
Aghia Galini................................33
Matala.........................................37
Iraklion .......................................41
Kokkini Hani ...............................48
Gouves ........................................50
Hersonissos.................................52
Stalis ..........................................57
Malia...........................................61
Aghios Nikolaos...........................65

**EXCURSIONS** ..............69
The Samaria Gorge ......................71
Gortys, Faistos &
    Aghia Triada...........................74
Knossos ......................................77
The Lasithi Plateau......................81
Santorini......................................83

**LIFESTYLE**.........................93
Food & drink ..............................94
Menu decoder .............................98
Shopping ...................................100
Children .....................................102
Sports & activities .....................104
Festivals & events.......................107

**PRACTICAL INFORMATION** ...109
Accommodation ........................110
Preparing to go .........................112
During your stay ........................116

**INDEX**.................................125

**MAPS**
Crete...........................................6
Chania.........................................14
Rethymnon..................................26
Iraklion.......................................40
Malia...........................................62
Aghios Nikolaos...........................66
Santorini......................................84

## WHAT'S IN YOUR GUIDEBOOK?

**Independent authors** Impartial, up-to-date information from our travel experts who meticulously source local knowledge.

**Experience** Thomas Cook's 165 years in the travel industry and guidebook publishing enriches every word with expertise you can trust.

**Travel know-how** Thomas Cook has thousands of staff working around the globe, all living and breathing travel.

**Editors** Travel-publishing professionals, pulling everything together to craft a perfect blend of words, pictures, maps and design.

**You, the traveller** We deliver a practical, no-nonsense approach to information, geared to how you really use it.

● *Watching the sun set over one of Crete's picturesque churches*

# INTRODUCTION
Getting to know Crete

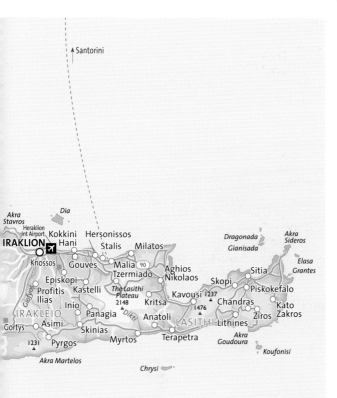

↑ Santorini

Akra
Stavros    Dia
Heraklion
Int Airport    Kokkini    Hersonissos    Dragonada    Akra
IRAKLION ○ ✈    Hani    Stalis    Milatos    Gianisada    Sideros
Knossos    Gouves    Malia 90    Aghios    Elasa
Episkopi    Tzermiado    Nikolaos    Skopi    Sitia    Grantes
Profitis    Kastelli    The Lasithi    Kavousi 1237    Piskokefalo
Ilias    Plateau    Kritsa    Chandras    Kato
Inio    2148 ▲    1476    Ziros    Zakros
IRAKLEIO    Panagia    Dikti    Anatoli    LASITHI    Lithines
Gortys ○ Asimi    Skinias    Terapeta    Akra
1231 ▲    Pyrgos    Myrtos    Goudoura
Akra Martelos    Koufonisi
Chrysi

Libyan Sea

Santorini

Crete

# Getting to know Crete

The largest and most southerly of all the Greek islands, Crete is a great all-round destination with attractive things to see and do for all travellers. It has both sandy beaches and world-class ancient ruins; a wicked clubbing scene and peaceful hikes among flowers; fish 'n' chips with beer, and gourmet Cretan specialities washed down with wine.

## GEOGRAPHY
Almost cigar-shaped, the island is 250 km (155 miles) long but fairly narrow. It is the most southerly part of Europe and is just 300 km (186 miles) off the coast of Africa. The island is dominated by the huge backbone of the White Mountains (Lefka Ori) in the west, the Mount Ida massif in the centre (this provides the highest peak – Psiloritis – at 2,456 m/8,058 ft) and the Lasithi Mountains towards the east. Gorges are a feature of these mountains. The most famous of these is the Samaria Gorge (see page 71), with its stark vertical rocks, which people flock to see all the year round.

## LIFESTYLE
The Cretans are farmers and fishermen at heart. Olives and vines, both labour-intensive crops at certain times of the year, remain central to the economy, but figs, almonds, citrus fruits, apricots and melons are also grown and eaten, and form the basis of the 'Mediterranean diet', considered to be the healthiest in the developed world.

## NATURE
In high summer the landscape looks parched, but come in spring and you'll find Crete to be green and filled with wild flowers. Hiking the fields and mountains is popular in spring and autumn (and you may spot a kri-kri goat or two). In autumn, the landscape is brightened by little white-flowered *Cyclamen creticum* and other bulbs. In spring, anemones fill the olive groves and more than 60 species of orchid can be found. There's life beyond the beaches too, and nearly anyone can try scuba

🔺 *Allow yourself to soak up Crete's atmosphere with regular café stops*

diving at a variety of resorts to see a glimpse of the rich life below
the waves.

## VILLAGES

It is very easy to slip away from the busy coastline and venture inland to
find enchanting, unspoilt villages where you can sit in a square shaded
by an ancient plane tree, just watching the world go by. Several
traditional villages have become particularly popular, including Kritsa,
near Aghios Nikolaos (see page 65); the fact that it is now a craft centre
adds to its undoubted charms. Mochos, on the way up to Lasithi
(see page 81), is another village with a good atmosphere.

# THE BEST OF CRETE

Whether it's lazing on the beach, surfing, fine dining, clubbing, hiking or seeing ancient cities, Crete has an amazing variety of things to see and do.

## TOP 10 ATTRACTIONS

- **Chania & Rethymnon** Stroll the narrow streets of Crete's two prettiest cities, and discover old churches, mosques, medieval houses and Venetian forts (see pages 15 and 27).

- **Faistos & Knossos** Explore the remains of the great Minoan culture at these famous palaces (see pages 74 and 77).

- **Lasithi Plateau** Drive up to this fertile plateau, which has been farmed for thousands of years, to see its many windmills and unique lifestyle (see page 81).

- **Samaria Gorge** For a huge sense of achievement, hike through Europe's most famous and spectacular gorge (see page 71).

- **Santorini** Visit this stunning island archipelago, world famous for its white cubist villages draped over dramatic volcanic cliffs (see page 83).

- **Underwater world** Explore life beneath the waves, either by scuba diving or on a glass-bottom boat tour in Chania or Aghios Nikolaos (see pages 16 and 67).

- **Elafonissi** Take a boat from Paleochora to the beautiful lagoon and beach at Elafonissi (see page 21).

- **Tourist train excursion** Take the children on a fun tourist train excursion from Platanias, visiting caves, gorges, villages or pretty bays (see page 23).

- **Matala** Visit the pretty beach and explore Roman-era caves in the nearby cliffs (see page 37).

- **Clubbing** Go wild at the many bars and clubs in the party towns of Hersonissos and Malia (see pages 56 and 64).

 *One of the frescoes at Knossos*

## SYMBOLS KEY

The following symbols are used throughout this book:

ⓐ address  ☎ telephone  ⓦ website address  ⓔ email
🕐 opening times  ❶ important

The following symbols are used on the maps:

| | | | |
|---|---|---|---|
| 🄸 information office | | ◯ | city |
| ✖ post office | | ◯ | large town |
| 🛍 shopping | | ○ | small town |
| ✈ airport | | ▪ | point of interest |
| ✚ hospital | | — | main road |
| 🛡 police station | | — | minor road |
| 🚌 bus station | | | |
| ✝ cathedral | | | |
| ❶ numbers denote featured cafés, restaurants & evening venues | | | |

### RESTAURANT CATEGORIES

The symbol after the name of each restaurant listed in this guide indicates the price of a typical main course plus starter or dessert and drink for one person.

£ under €12   ££ €12–25   £££ over €25

❶ *Chania's elegant harbour*

# RESORTS
Places under the sun

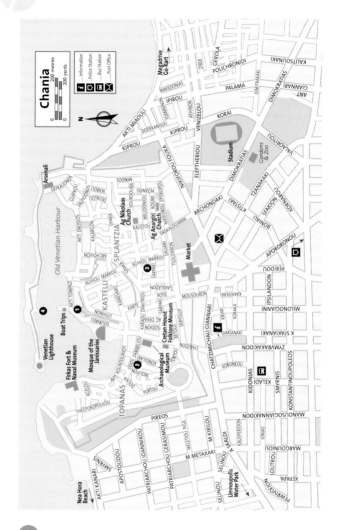

# Chania

The focal point for exploration in charming Chania (pronounced 'Han-ya') is the elegant Venetian harbour, with its colour-washed façades and buzzing café atmosphere. The town is also renowned for its atmospheric old quarter, fort and museums. You can shop for souvenirs in the narrow streets behind the harbour, and seek out the famous Leather Alley – or inspect the delicious local produce on sale in the bustling covered market.

Chania's Venetian harbourfront is ringed by cafés, bars and restaurants, behind which runs Zambeliou, the street that leads into the heart of the old quarter. Search here for souvenirs or lunch in one of the atmospheric tavernas, found among the tangle of narrow alleyways. Alternatively, snack on fresh bread or a *tiropitákia* (small pastry filled with cheese) from the wood-burning *fournos* (bakery) on Theotokopoulou. **Firkas Fort** and the **Naval Museum** (see page 16) stand guard at the western end of the harbour, while Kastelli, at the eastern end, is the site of the earliest settlement in Chania. Below Kastelli Hill, the domes of the Mosque of the Janissaries form a feature at the harbour edge. Walk around the mosque to the inner harbour to view the remains of the Venetian Arsenali (dry docks). If you're energetic, you could walk all the way around the harbour to the lighthouse on the pier. Good views of the harbour and town can be had from Kastelli Hill and from the fortress. Apart from the busy shopping streets around Athinagora Square, the old town has numerous alleys that are perfect for ambling around. In parts of the old town, especially in the Splantzia district in the eastern part of the old town, where old mosque minarets stand between crumbling houses, it's like time has stood still.

## BEACHES

The nearest beach, **Nea Hora**, is a short walk beyond Firkas Fort, and has cafés and restaurants.

## THINGS TO SEE & DO

### Archaeological Museum

The former Venetian Church of San Francesco, once the island's grandest
building, makes an ideal setting for Minoan storage jars, wonderfully
decorated clay coffins, sculptures, glassware and mosaics from Greek
and Roman times.

ⓐ Odos Chalidon 21 ⓣ 28210 90334 ⓛ 08.00–20.00 Tues–Sun (all year);
13.30–20.00 Mon (summer only) ⓘ Admission charge

### Boat trips

Boat trips include excursions to the island of Theodorou, home of the
native wild goat and ancient city of Akitos. Other boats go to Doru, Theo
and the Lazaretta islands. Try the glass-bottom submarine boat for
unforgettable views of the seabed and the wreckage of a World War II
aeroplane.

### Cretan House Folklore Museum

A fun museum where kids and adults can learn about traditional Cretan
crafts. Mrs Bikaki makes and sells impressive embroideries depicting
village scenes.

ⓐ Odos Chalidon 46B ⓣ 28210 90816 ⓛ 09.00–15.00, 18.00–21.00
Mon–Sat, closed Sun ⓘ Admission charge

### Diving

Divers can discover a Chania as beautiful below the water as it is
above. One of many diving centres, **Blue Adventures Diving**, caters for
all abilities.

ⓐ Odos Archoleon 11 ⓣ 28210 40608 ⓦ www.blueadventuresdiving.gr

### Firkas Fort & Naval Museum

Wander freely around Firkas Fort before visiting the museum. Inside is a
superb model of Venetian-era Chania, detailed models of boats through
the ages and a poignant exhibition about the first airborne invasion,

during the 1941 Battle of Crete, and the first submarine attack in history.
ⓐ Akti Kountourioti ☎ 28210 91875 ⏰ 09.00–21.00 (summer);
08.30–15.00 (winter) ⓘ Small charge

## Horse & carriage rides

Drive around Chania in style. The starting point is from beside the
Mosque of the Janissaries.

🔺 *A courtyard in Chania's old town*

### Limnoupolis Water Park

Plenty of fun here to keep the family entertained, from water slides and swimming pools to the climbing wall, playgrounds, shops and restaurants. ⓐ 8 km (5 miles) west of Chania on the road to Omalos ⓣ 28210 33246 ⓦ www.limnoupolis.gr ⓛ 10.00–18.00 ⓘ Admission charge

### Megadrive Go-Kart

A large track with karts for adults and children, and even two-seaters. ⓐ On the road to Mournies ⓣ 28210 97533 ⓦ www.megadrive-gokart.gr ⓛ 09.00–22.00

## TAKING A BREAK

The harbourside restaurants have the best views and atmosphere but are more expensive than tavernas in the old town behind. Head beyond the Arsenali to the end of the inner harbour for the best fish tavernas.

**Monastiri £ ❶** This harbourside taverna serves authentic Cretan dishes. ⓐ Akti Tompazi 12 ⓣ 28210 55527 ⓦ www.monastiri-taverna.gr ⓛ 12.00–23.00

**Tamam ££ ❷** Housed in an atmospheric former Turkish bath inside a 16th-century building in the heart of the old quarter, this excellent taverna is always busy. Make sure you get there early, or be prepared to wait. ⓐ Odos Zambeliou 49 ⓣ 28210 96080 ⓛ 19.30–00.30

> ### SHOPPING
> Chania's covered market is a swirl of colour, with massed displays of every kind of produce imaginable, including local honey with nuts, herbs and spices, and the cheese for which the area is famed. Leather Alley (Skrydlof) is the place to buy belts, handbags and sandals, or even a pair of made-to-order, traditional Cretan boots.

**Well of the Turk ££ ❸**   Tucked away in a maze of lanes in the old Splantzia district, this is a delightful place away from the busy port. It serves good Middle Eastern, Cretan and Greek food. Be sure to see the well and the fountain with scenes from Istanbul. ⓐ Odos Kallinikou Sarpaki 1–3 ❶ 28210 54547 ⓦ www.welloftheturk.com ❶ 19.30–late Wed–Sun, closed Mon & Tues

**Forteza £££ ❹**   Restaurants do not come much more romantic than this one. It is set in the sea wall next to the lighthouse. A free ferry shuttles people across from the harbour, otherwise it would be a long walk round. They serve an international cuisine that is a bit pricey but worth the expense for a special occasion. ⓐ Old Venetian harbour ❶ 28210 41550 ❶ 11.00–24.00

▲ *Cafés and restaurants line Chania's harbour*

# Paleochora

Once home to a grand Venetian castle, Paleochora is a pretty village straddling a peninsula in the southwest of Crete. The quiet main avenue is lined with eucalyptus trees, underneath which are a few bars and tavernas.

The town beaches are on either side of the village. There are two beaches: to the west, a long stretch of sandy beach, and to the east, a pebbly coastline ideal for snorkelling. It is not a busy resort, being such a long drive from anywhere, but the main Venizelos Street does wake up in the evening as the atmospheric bars and restaurants start to come alive.

## BEACHES

The largest and best beach is to the west and is simply called Sandy Beach. It is wide and equipped with every facility. The reliable winds make it an excellent spot for windsurfer enthusiasts, though there's currently no rental outlet. Pebble Beach, to the east, has stones and is not as pretty as the opposite bay, but this is where you will find the harbour and a busy promenade lined with restaurants.

## THINGS TO SEE & DO

### Acritans of Europe Museum
A new exhibition about Crete and other borderlands between Europe and the Middle East, where besides conflicts there were many cultural exchanges, resulting in epic poetry that was once known across Europe.
🕿 28230 42265 🕘 10.00–13.00, 18.30–21.00 Wed–Sun, closed Mon & Tues

### Boat trips
Several boat companies offer cruises to nearby villages and beaches, or dolphin-spotting trips. An evening sail to nearby Temenia with its ancient church followed by dinner in Azoghires is also popular.

### Elafonissi

A path following the coastline west of Paleochora leads all the way to Elafonissi, a small town with a tropical lagoon and beautiful sandy beaches. You can walk there in the cool morning in about 2–3 hours and arrange a boat to bring you back, or hop on one of the daily boat and bus tours. Elafonissi is actually an island, but the waters to it are shallow and it is only a short wade across the sandbar.

### Fortress

To the south of Paleochora you can climb up to the fort. There is not much here apart from the old walls of the castle of Selinos, built by the Venetians in 1279. The hike is worth it for the views over the peninsula.

### Sougia & Lissos

Another worthwhile trip, this time to the east of Paleochora. Sougia is a small village with many simple restaurants and bars around a huge bay of the cleanest, clearest waters. Combine your trip with a visit to the ruins of ancient Lissos.

## TAKING A BREAK

**Café Almyrida £** Greek and Western snacks and breakfasts, salads and home-made cakes can be enjoyed in this simple café with a terrace.
ⓐ Village centre ⓣ 28230 41308 ⓛ 08.30–22.30

**Pizzeria Niki £** A popular pizza restaurant, also serving Greek dishes. Situated near Sandy Beach, it is set in a lovely courtyard with trees and flowers, and has more than enough room for tourists and locals.
ⓣ 28230 41532 ⓛ 11.00–15.00, 18.00–23.00

**The Third Eye £** Vegetarian restaurants are unusual in Greece. This one has a daily-changing menu of Greek, Asian and European dishes.
ⓐ On an unnamed street near Sandy Beach ⓣ 28230 41234
ⓦ www.thethirdeye-paleochora.com ⓛ 08.00–15.30, 17.30–23.30

# Aghia Marina & Platanias

Just west of Chania lies a string of idyllic resorts where the pace of life is anything but stressful. It starts with Aghia Marina, a friendly resort blessed with one of the best beaches in the area. Aghia Marina seems to run into Platanias, and the two could almost be classed as one long resort, but Platanias is the more lively of the two, and this is where you will find most of the shops and restaurants.

The whole coastline here has a good selection of sandy beaches and all are conveniently connected to one another by the busy coastal road with its excellent bus connections to and from Chania. Shops, restaurants, and a wealth of things to see and do, make this an area people return to each year.

## BEACHES

Aghia Marina and Platanias are the focal points of a continuous development west of Chania that follows the coast road around the

▲ *View of Aghia Marina from Stalos*

beautiful bay edged with sand-and-shingle beach most of the way. Aghia Marina itself lies about 9 km (6 miles) from Chania, and has one of the best stretches of sand, with bars, tavernas, nightlife, low-rise accommodation and watersports hire facilities. Some 3 km (2 miles) further along the coast road, livelier Platanias has a less-sandy beach.

## THINGS TO SEE & DO

### Active excursions

Treks on foot or by mountain bike, as well as kayaking, rapelling, canyoning and more, are organised by **Trekking Plan**. This company also takes groups on walks down the Imbros Gorge, south of Chania.

ⓐ Beside the Santa Marina Hotel ⓣ 28210 60861 ⓦ www.cycling.gr

### Cycle in the hills

There are several bike-hire shops in the resort, from where the adventurous can explore the steep little lanes among the olive groves that rise on the hills behind the resorts. In just minutes, you have fabulous views out to sea and along the coast well beyond the city of Chania.

### Little Fun Train

Platanias is the main station for the tourist trains that offer seven different 2–3-hour excursions in the area, with stops at caves, gorges, raki breweries, quiet villages and quaint bays. Three of the tours also pass through Aghia Marina. Morning and evening departures.

ⓣ 28210 60817 ⓘ Admission charge

### Smile Park

A small but fun playground for children with a bouncy castle, slides, swings and a go-kart track. There's a bar for the adults to relax and keep an eye on the fun.

ⓐ Between Aghia Marina and Platanias, main road ⓣ 28210 60700
ⓒ 17.00–22.00 ⓘ Small charge for the rides

## DRIVING EXCURSION

The drive on to the Rodopou peninsula up from the charming fishing village of Kolymbari is well worth it for the views back along the rocky coastline with Chania in the distance. The road loops back upon itself. Halfway along is the tiny town of Afrata, where you will find a few simple tavernas as well as a road that leads to a secret rocky cove.

The road south from Kolymbari climbs up towards Episkopi, where there are two unique churches. Past the town of Spilia is a sign on the right, pointing to the **Chapel of Aghios Stefanos**, a tiny 10th-century white-walled building sheltering below oak trees. The key should be in the door. Inside, the chapel's walls are decorated with beautiful frescoes.

Further on from here, and signposted, is the much larger **Church of Mihail Arhangelos Episkopi**, one of the oldest churches in Greece, with a unique dome. It has been suggested that the centre rotunda dates back to the first Byzantine period in the 6th century. The church is not always open but a guardian monk lives on-site, and you may be able to find him and ask to see the impressive frescoes inside dating back to the 10th century.

## TAKING A BREAK

**Balau £** A lovely tropical-style beach bar set between tall palm trees. Serves beers, cocktails and snacks, and rents out beach chairs and parasols. ❸ Aghia Marina beach, near the church ● 09.00–03.00

**Dodoni £** Fantastic home-made ice cream, coffee, pastries and waffles. A popular place to cool down after roasting on the beach or after dinner. ❸ Platanias, main square ● 10.00–23.00

**Kantari £–££** Waiters at this popular taverna do not hassle clients at the entrance, so you can take your time to read through the large Greek and international menu before taking a table in this lovely vine-covered garden set away from the road. ❸ Platanias, main road ❶ 28210 68090 ● 12.00–23.00

**Haroupia ££** Set on the hill directly behind Platanias' main square, Haroupia is an excellent tavern serving Greek food, grilled specialities and Cretan pies. The terrace beneath the beautiful roof offers great views over the town and sea. ⓐ Platanias ⓣ 28210 68603 ⓛ 10.00–23.00

**Mitsos ££** Overlooking the Agii Theodore bay, this beachside restaurant serves breakfast through to dinner. Specialities include delicious meat and fish dishes grilled over charcoal. Services include Wi-Fi. ⓐ Aghia Marina ⓣ 28210 68494 ⓛ 09.00–23.00

**Mylos tou Kerata £££** This excellent restaurant was converted from a 14th-century watermill, and is tastefully decorated in traditional village style, complete with trees and a duck pond. Waiters will go out of their way to make your meal memorable, organising special requests like flowers and champagne. One of the best restaurants on Crete. ⓐ Platanias, main road ⓣ 28210 68578 ⓦ www.mylos-tou-kerata.gr ⓛ 18.00–01.00 ❗ Book ahead

## AFTER DARK

There is a nightly exodus from Aghia Marina and Platanias to Chania as people go there for a meal before heading back for late-night drinks and dancing nearer to their hotels.

**All Bar One** The friendliest bar in Aghia Marina is run by Mark and Tracy from the UK, who create a sophisticated chilled-out atmosphere for guests to enjoy their beer or cocktails. Regular events include quiz and film nights. ⓐ Aghia Marina, main road beside Haris Hotel ⓣ 69426 12878 ⓛ 18.00–04.00

**Utopia** One of the best nightlife options in Platanias, with a well-designed tropical-style bar, a pleasant café and a new club in the basement. ⓐ Platanias, main road ⓣ 28210 60033 ⓛ 10.00–05.00

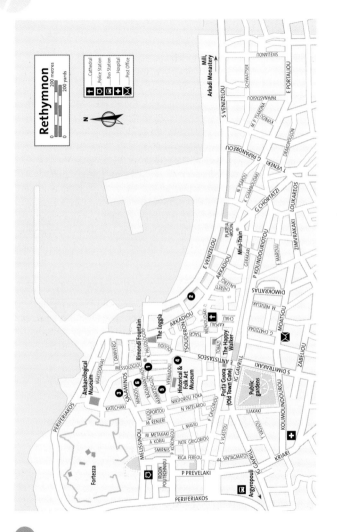

# Rethymnon

Stealing all the attention in the vibrant resort of Rethymnon is the old Venetian town that lies at its heart. A maze of narrow alleyways, with a fascinating blend of Venetian and Turkish architecture, an atmospheric harbour and a huge Venetian fortress all combine in a relatively small area to make this one of the most interesting towns on Crete.

Seductive by night, Venetian façades and bustling tavernas line the intimate fishing harbour. Close by, up on the hill above the harbour, are the imposing Venetian fortress and the Archaeological Museum, watching over the narrow streets of the old town.

Just 5 km (3 miles) from Rethymnon is Platanes (not to be confused with the town of Platanias near Aghia Marina), a perfect base for many of the area's main attractions. For a small town, it has a fair share of restaurants, bars and nightlife. The main beach road allows good access to both east and west coastlines.

## BEACHES

The town centre fronts directly on to a sandy beach with reasonable facilities, though it is sometimes crowded and dirty, and has dangerous undercurrents when the red flag is flying. For cleaner stretches, head to Platanes, 5 km (3 miles) east, where there is no shortage of sunbeds, umbrellas and water-based activities.

## THINGS TO SEE & DO

### Archaeological Museum
Built by the Turks as an extra defence for the fort, the building later became a prison, and is now a museum. It has a small but interesting collection of local Minoan, Greek and Roman finds. The Minoan statuary and painted clay coffins are particularly worth a look, as is the Roman jewellery. ⓐ Opposite the fortress entrance ⓣ 28310 54668 ⓛ 08.30–15.00 Tues–Sun, closed Mon ⓘ Admission charge

### Boat trips

Although there are long day trips to Santorini from here (see page 83), you can also stay closer to home on a full day trip with **Dolphin Cruises** (❶ 28310 57666 Ⓦ www.dolphin-cruises.com). Board the *Barbarossa* for a cruise along the western coastline to Marathi, taking in pirate caves and a swimming stop. Alternatively, go fishing on the *Albatross* or on a trip to Panormo village. The 'Captain Hook pirate ship' cruise sails east along the coast to the caves at Skaleta and the Camarola Arch, returning via the Fortezza. There are also regular 'sunset and stars' trips. You're not guaranteed to see dolphins, but the company promises half your cash back if the boat sinks. Boats sail from the Venetian harbour.

### Diving

Several diving companies offer diving options, including PADI courses at the excellent **Paradise Diving Centre** (❶ 28310 26317 Ⓦ www.diving-center.gr). They're based just out of town in Petres but have a pick-up service.

### Fortezza

The large 16th-century Venetian fortress failed to prevent the Turks from taking over the town in 1646. They turned the Catholic cathedral inside the fortress into a mosque with an impressive dome, which still remains today with several churches, houses, gunpowder magazines and excellent views.

ⓐ Odos Salaminos ❶ 28310 28101 ❶ 08.00–19.00 (summer); 08.30–15.00 (winter) ❶ Admission charge

### Historical & Folk Art Museum

Recently resited in a 17th-century mansion, this is one for all the family – a fascinating collection of implements connected with traditional crafts, household goods, costumes and jewellery. It shows how everyday life changed very little in the centuries from the time of Venetian rule until relatively recently.

ⓐ Odos Vernadou 28–30 ❶ 28310 23398 ❶ 10.00–14.30 Mon–Sat, closed Sun ❶ Admission charge

### The Loggia

This building is one of the most brilliant examples of Renaissance architecture in Crete. Originally used by the Venetian public authorities, it also served as a meeting place for the city's nobility. It is now an upmarket art shop.

❷ On the corner of Arkadiou and Paleologou 2

### Mini-Train

❷ Starts from Plateia Iroon and makes a circuit round town.

🕒 Every half-hour, 10.00–23.00 ❶ Half-price for 3- to 12-year-olds

### Porta Guora (Old Town Gate)

The only surviving gate of the ancient city walls. The nearby Public Gardens host a lively wine festival in the last two weeks of July.

### Rimondi Fountain

Three lions' heads spout water from this ancient fountain, the focal point of life in the old quarter.

🔺 *Colourful boats decorate Rethymnon's bustling harbour*

## Walking

The **Happy Walker** offers a choice of seven easy to demanding guided walks through fields of flowers, gorges and villages, followed by lunch in a local taverna. Also arranges full walking holidays.

ⓐ Odos Tobazi 56 ☎ 28310 52920 ⓦ www.happywalker.com

🕐 17.00–20.30 Sun–Fri, closed Sat (Mar–Nov)

## DRIVING EXCURSIONS

### Argyropouli

This is a tranquil town, to the west of Rethymnon, with freshwater springs that are the source of water for the area. A good place for lunch and a refreshing drink.

### Arkadi Monastery

This old, fort-like monastery, its history tied up with the Cretan struggle for independence, enjoys a great location in the hills. If driving, be sure to return via the characterful villages of Eleftherna and Margarites.

🕐 08.00–13.00, 15.30–19.00 ❶ Small admission charge

### Mili

Five kilometres (3 miles) east of Rethymnon there is a turning to this deserted pretty village that is well worth a visit.

## TAKING A BREAK

**La Creperie £** ❶ Within sight of the Rimondi fountain, this cheap fast-food restaurant offers good-quality sweet and savoury pancakes. See the daily specials board. You can sit inside or opt for a takeaway.

ⓐ Odos Arabatzoglou 10 ☎ 28310 50230 🕐 10.00–23.00

**Samaria £** ❷ One of the best of the seafront tavernas, with tables outdoors and an array of tasty Greek meat and fish dishes.

ⓐ Odos E Venizelou 39–40 ☎ 28310 24681 🕐 09.00–24.00

### SAVE THE TURTLES

The loggerhead sea turtle, which lives only in the Mediterranean, is now on the brink of extinction. Between June and September turtles use the beaches near Chania, Rethymnon and Messara Bay as their hatching grounds. Archelon, the sea turtle protection society, patrols the beaches, monitors nests and informs visitors how to help protect turtles. For more information see Ⓦ www.archelon.gr

**Alana ££** ❸  A traditional taverna in the heart of the old town. Serves Cretan dishes and wine. ⓐ Odos Salaminos ❶ 28310 27737 ⓛ 11.00–23.00

**Lemonokipos ££** ❹  The 'Lemon Tree Garden' taverna has tables set under fragrant lemon trees; its varied menu has good Cretan specialities. ⓐ Odos E Antistaseos 100 ❶ 28310 57087 ⓛ 09.00–23.00

**Veneto ££–£££** ❺  Spectacularly set in a building that was once a 14th-century monastery and later a 16th-century Venetian palace. The inside is stunning, as is the tempting, secluded courtyard around the back. For a Cretan speciality, order the goat with *stamnagathi* (local wild herbs). ⓐ Odos Epimenidou 4, off Vernadou ❶ 28310 56634 Ⓦ www.veneto.gr ⓛ 09.00–24.00

**Avli Restaurant £££** ❻  Eat inside the 17th-century Venetian manor house underneath curved cellar walls or outside in the pretty courtyard for a memorable upmarket meal. ⓐ Odos Xanthoudidou 22, off Radamanthios ❶ 28310 58250 Ⓦ www.avli.gr ⓛ 12.00–23.00

### AFTER DARK

Nightlife revolves around the streets of the old quarter, the Venetian harbour and the seafront road. The harbour road to Iroon Square is closed to traffic every evening.

◆ *The pretty hillside town of Aghia Galini*

# Aghia Galini

Squeezed in on three sides by a huge mountain range at the foot of the Amari Valley, Aghia Galini has grown up from a remote fishing village into a popular resort. As you enter Aghia Galini the sign reading 'Welcome home' shows the popularity with British holidaymakers of this laid-back resort. Many return year after year, especially in the shoulder seasons. The town's narrow streets are lined with white houses and the usual restaurants and tavernas. The buildings appear to tumble down from the hill towards the pretty harbour.

## BEACHES

The main town beach, with its tavernas, parasols, sunbeds and clear waters, is reached by a footpath from the harbour, or by car from the main road. On the beach, **Ioannis Minadakis** ( 28320 91147) offers a variety of watersports rentals.

### Aghios Georgios
It is possible to walk to this shingle cove, but the boat will be much easier. It is a great place to relax and take an easy lunch at one of the two tavernas. Water taxis are available from the harbour.

### Aghios Pavlos
Further away than Aghios Georgios and more attractive with its sheltered bay, impressive rock formations and good snorkelling. There is another beach near here that can be reached by walking west over the headland. Water taxis are available from the harbour.

## THINGS TO SEE & DO

### Cruises
There are daily cruises from Aghia Galini to many nearby islands and beaches. Paximadia Island, 12 km (7½ miles) offshore, is worth a visit for

its lovely sandy beaches. Fishing is also good on this side of Crete, and boat excursions offer the chance to catch and grill your own lunch. Book tickets in advance at the boats or from any travel agent.

The *Elisabeth* sails past (and into) some pretty caves to an isolated beach where you can barbecue the fish you caught yourself!

ⓐ Argonaftis ① 28320 91346

## TAKING A BREAK

**Café Platia £** A fantastic little café, bistro and wine bar on the village square just behind the harbour. Enjoy healthy breakfasts, fresh fruit juice, ice cream, tapas and salads. ① 28320 91185 🕒 08.00–14.00, 18.00–02.00

**Alexander Bar ££** Just below Madame Hortense, this lounge bar serves breakfast, snacks and cocktails to relaxed music. Sports events are screened on TV; there's Internet access, and DJs play at night.
① 28320 91226 🕒 08.00–23.00

## AFTER DARK

### RESTAURANTS
**Kostas ££** Great views over the harbour, friendly service and a good Greek menu, with tempting fish specialities. ① 28320 91323 🕒 12.00–02.00

**Madame Hortense ££** A rooftop restaurant with flowers winding their way along the balcony and some great photos of old Aghia Galini. Try Mediterranean specialities such as the chicken fillet served with a sauce of seasonal fruits. ① 28320 91351 🕒 12.00–15.00, 18.00–01.00

### BAR
**Milestone** An excellent blues and jazz bar on Taverna Street run by English expat Gary Collyer. Request any song you like from the huge CD collection. ① 28230 91519 🕒 16.30–04.00

⬥ *Aghia Galini's beach is a few minutes' walk from the village*

⬥ The view from one of the caves that overlook the beach at Matala

# Matala

Honey-coloured cliffs dotted with caves that overlook a long curvaceous beach have made this town famous. These Roman or early Christian burial tombs were hippy hangouts in the 1960s. Famous names such as Cat Stevens and Bob Dylan are said to have lived in the caves. Matala is now a busy resort, attracting tourists by the busload. It is only a small town and visitors mainly come for the beautiful sandy beach. A single main road leads into the resort, then curves around into the old town, which is packed with souvenir shops, food stalls, currency exchanges and travel agents. Matala can get busy during the early afternoon, but if you get here in the morning or wait until the crowds have gone, you will find it magical to stare out towards the caves, watching the sun set, armed with your favourite cocktail.

## BEACHES

The main beach below the caves is the centre of attraction for visitors to Matala. The sea here is very good for swimming, if a little rough at times. The rocks by the caves make a convenient platform for divers, and snorkelling is also popular because the water is full of brightly coloured fish. Showers, toilets, changing rooms and parasols are provided. The beach has blue-flag status in recognition of its eco projects and commitment to sustainable development. At the back of the beach, trees provide some welcome shelter from the sun. If the beach is too crowded, consider walking 30 minutes south over the hill to Red Beach with its dark red sand (and some nudists), or head north to the spacious beaches at Komo and Kalamaki near Pitsidia (see page 39).

## THINGS TO SEE & DO

### The caves
You can wander around the fascinating cliffs and caves freely, though the area is now fenced off and locked up at night to discourage people

from having parties here. The caves are well worth looking around for their elaborate décor. Inside are carved windows, seats and benches. During World War II, the caves doubled as munitions dumps, and then in the 1960s a large foreign community gathered here.

### Melanouri Horse Farm

On the main road into Matala is the village of Pitsidia (see opposite), where this ranch is situated. There are organised rides for all abilities of horsemanship. The trip through the olive groves to neighbouring villages sounds marvellous, as does the sunset ride on Komo beach. A picnic of olives, bread, cheeses and wine is provided.

🕿 28920 45040 🌐 www.melanouri.com 🖂 info@melanouri.com

🔺 *Rock-cut tombs at Matala*

## Pitsidia

A few kilometres north along the main road to Matala, Pitsidia village is less hectic in high season and arguably has better beaches. To the north is Kalamaki, a long, empty beach with a few places to eat. Komo beach with its single snack bar and parasol rental is a short drive to the west. Right beside the beach, archaeologists are in the process of unearthing a complete Minoan-era harbour town. The site is not open yet, but you can peer through the fences to get an idea.

## TAKING A BREAK

**Corali £** This restaurant offers breakfast and a good selection of steaks, grills and Greek specialities. ⓐ Main square ⓣ 28920 45744 ⓦ www.corali-matala.com ⓛ 08.00–01.00

**Skala Fish Tavern £** This small, family-run restaurant serves traditional Greek food. It is very cosy and has the most fantastic views to the cliffs and caves. Mrs Maria does all the cooking and her daughter helps in the restaurant. ⓐ A short walk south around the bay, through a bar and up some uneven steps ⓣ 28920 45489 ⓛ 09.00–late ❶ Cash only

**Waves £** A reasonably priced restaurant overlooking the beach, serving fish and meat that is all cooked on the barbecue. Try *à la chef* – chicken served with a mushroom, paprika and cream sauce. ⓣ 28920 45361 ⓛ 09.30–01.00 ❶ Visa and MasterCard accepted

**Zouridakis Bakery £** Delicious cakes, sandwiches, pastries and home-made ice cream. ⓐ Village square ⓣ 28920 45450 ⓦ www.zouridakis.gr ⓛ 08.00–23.00

## AFTER DARK

**Karnagio Club** At the very end of the village, this club has open sea views and a bar hewn into a cave. ⓣ 28210 53366 ⓛ 12.00–03.00

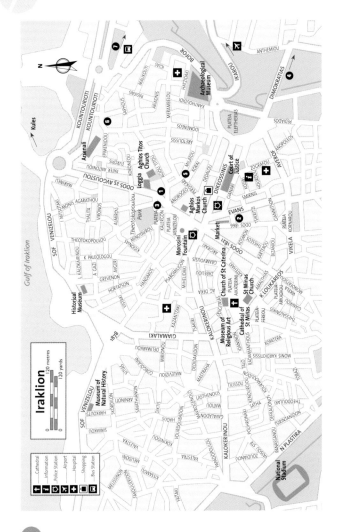

# Iraklion

Your first taste of present-day Iraklion, the capital of Crete and the fifth-largest city in Greece, will give you little idea of the treasures behind its ancient walls. Dusty, bustling and noisy, Iraklion is easy to dislike, but hidden within a relatively compact area you will find some of the best shopping around, a lively street market, cafés set in leafy squares and one of the most important collections of archaeological finds in all of Greece. Children, especially, will love the castle down by the tranquil marina.

Start a tour of the sights at the small fishing harbour/marina, alongside the **Venetian Arsenali**, the dry docks where ships were once overhauled and built. Visit the Venetian Fort (see page 44), before heading up 25th Avgoustou Street (Odos 25 Avgoustou) into the city centre. (A short diversion from here leads to the **Historical Museum** of Crete – see page 43.) Note that 25th Avgoustou (the main road from port to town) is closed to cars.

Watch out for **Aghios Titos Church**, set back in the square on the left. Built during the Byzantine era, then rebuilt by the Venetians, it served time as a Turkish mosque before being converted back to Christian use in 1925. Its prize possession is a reliquary containing the skull of St Titos, an important saint on the island. The shaded café here makes an inviting coffee stop.

A classic arcade announces the **Loggia** (Town Hall), once a meeting place for Venetian nobility, before you pass **Aghios Markos Church** and enter the bustling hub of Venizelou Square (Plateia Venizelou), with its outdoor cafés and **Morosini Fountain**. The structure was named after Francesco Morosini, who was governor in 1627 when it was built, but the lions on the fountain predate the rest of it by a few hundred years.

Odos 1866, a lively, pedestrianised street, and home to the **Saturday morning market**, leads to Kornarou Square (Plateia Kornarou), with a Turkish pumphouse, now a café, and the **Bembo Fountain**. Turn right here, then round and down Kyrilou Loukareos to the **Cathedral of St Minas**. Pass to the left and alongside the older **Church of St Caterina**

◆ The cooling Morosini fountain in Iraklion

**SHOPPING**

Elegant shops line the streets of Dikeossinis and Dedalou (near the Morosini Fountain), and the shops around Odos 1821 and Plateia Venizelou are worth a look. There is a huge Saturday market by the bus station near the city's port.

behind the cathedral. Clothes shops begin to feature more strongly now as the route meets Odos 1821 and goes left back to Plateia Venizelou. Shopaholics might fancy a foray along Dikeossinis. The main route continues right into Dedalou, opposite the Morosini Fountain, a mecca for serious shoppers. Emerge into the expanse of Plateia Eleftherias, where the large yellow building to the left houses Iraklion's **Archaeological Museum**, which specialises in Minoan artefacts.

## THINGS TO SEE & DO

### Archaeological Museum

The museum houses the most important collection of Minoan finds anywhere in the world, and a visit will greatly enhance excursions to Knossos and other sites on the island. Artefacts and frescoes give a good insight into the everyday life of the Minoans, as well as the ancient Greeks and Romans. The museum is being renovated and only highlights of the collection are on show until 2012.

ⓐ Plateia Eleftherias ❶ 28102 26092 ❷ 13.30–20.00 Mon, 08.00–20.00 Tues–Sun (summer); 08.00–19.30 Tues–Sun, closed Mon (winter)
❶ Admission charge; combined tickets with Knossos available

### Historical Museum

A must for museum buffs, this museum provides the opportunity to view artefacts from the Byzantine, Venetian and Turkish periods. Also housed in the museum is the library and study of Nikos Kazantzakis, author of *Zorba the Greek*, as well as relics of the Battle of Crete, a selection of folk art and a re-creation of the interior of a Cretan farmhouse.

ⓐ Odos Lysimachou Kalokairinou 7 ⓣ 28102 88708 ⓛ 09.00–17.00 Mon–Sat (summer); 08.30–15.00 Mon–Sat (winter), closed Sun ⓘ Admission charge

## Kules (Venetian Fort)

Superb views can be had from the ramparts of the renovated 16th-century Rocca al Mare, still known by its Turkish name of Kules. The internal rooms are intact and a few cannons and a collection of cannonballs lie scattered around to add to the atmosphere.

ⓐ Venetian harbour ⓛ 08.30–15.00 daily (summer); 08.30–15.00 Mon–Sat, closed Sun (winter) ⓘ Admission charge

## Museum of Natural History

Although small, this museum on the outskirts of the town has a fascinating collection of fossilised marine life and mounted animals that once lived on and around Crete.

ⓐ Leoforos Sofokli Venizelou ⓣ 28102 82740 ⓛ 08.00–20.00 Tues–Sun, closed Mon ⓘ Admission charge

## Museum of Religious Art

At the bottom of the square that also houses the impressive 19th-century Cathedral of St Minas and the original, medieval St Minas Church, the Aghia Ekaterini (Church of St Caterina) has been transformed into a museum of religious art. The walls are hung with impressive Cretan icons and reliquary objects.

ⓐ Plateia Aikaterini ⓣ 28102 88825 ⓛ 09.30–19.30 daily (summer); 08.30–15.00 Tues–Sun, closed Mon (winter) ⓘ Admission charge

## EXCURSION

### Fodele

Claimed by some as the birthplace of Crete's most famous artist, El Greco, Fodele is also a very pretty town lying just inland from the main coastal road, 30 km (19 miles) west of Iraklion. It's a good place to buy

△ *Kules: Iraklion's Venetian fort*

handmade local embroidery or to just relax in a shady café. North of the main road, flanked on both sides by mountains, is Fodele's beach, a large sandy cove with sunbeds, parasols and watersports facilities.

Back in Fodele, you can visit **El Greco's house and museum** (☎ 28105 21500 ● 09.00–17.00 Tues–Sun, closed Mon ❶ Admission charge), which is signposted across a bridge at the entrance into town. Nearby stands the 14th-century **Church of the Panayia** (● same times as the museum), which was built over an 8th-century basilica and still has outstanding 13th- and 14th-century frescoes inside.

## TAKING A BREAK

Crete's capital has a wide choice of places to eat and an abundance of pavement cafés and restaurants.

**Chicken Souvlaki £ ❶**  Signposted only in Greek next to the Loggia, this snack bar is perfect for a quick snack, with some of the best kebabs in Crete. No menu – just watch what the locals are ordering and ask for the same! ⓐ Odos 25 Avgoustou ● 09.00–03.00

**Giakoumis £ ❷**  This unassuming place is in a tiny covered alley off the main market, among similar-looking cafés. Seek it out for the grilled dishes: veal, steaks, pork, lamb chops and the best meatballs in Crete. ⓐ Odos Theodosaki 5–8, off Evans ☎ 28102 80277 ● 07.00–22.00 Mon–Sat, closed Sun

**Central Park ££ ❸**  A pleasant, modern café serving coffee, snacks and light meals. ⓐ Theotokopoulou Park ☎ 28103 46500 ● 08.00–02.00

## AFTER DARK

### RESTAURANTS

**O Kyriakos ££ ❹**  Famed home-style cooking in a quaint restaurant located just east of the town centre, with great lamb, stuffed aubergine

and local rocket salad. @ Leoforos Dimokratias 53 ❶ 28102 22464
🕒 10.00–23.00

**Loukoulos £££** ❺  Possibly the best restaurant in Crete, this is certainly
a good place to impress with its well-designed classic interior and courtyard shaded by lime trees. The Mediterranean dishes and salads on offer
are made with local organic ingredients. @ Odos Korai 5 ❶ 28102 24435
Ⓦ www.loukoulos-restaurant.gr 🕒 12.00–01.00

## BARS & CLUBS
The best bars are in Plateia Korai, a pleasant square behind Dedalou, and
in the more touristy area around Plateia Venizelou. There are not many
nightclubs in the city centre, but there are plenty of bars with loud music
and occasional dancing. Just follow the crowds!

**Café Veneto** ❻  A recent addition to Iraklion's nightlife options, this is a
modern bar and café that's popular with a young crowd, and gets very
busy at weekends. Nice views over the harbour and fortress.
@ Odos Epimenidou 9 ❶ 28102 23686

**Zig Zag** ❼  A popular bar and nightclub that serves up famed cocktails
in the evenings, with music genres from R&B to trance. You can also
order Mediterranean food. @ Odos Malia ❶ 28103 43344
🕒 12.00–02.00

# Kokkini Hani

Handily situated for Iraklion, Kokkini Hani (also known as Hani Kokkini) is a small resort along the old national road, now bypassed by the new highway. If you don't mind the planes flying overhead, the long, narrow stretch of sandy beach is great for relaxing, and it's well served with loungers and parasols and with all necessary facilities to hand. Most shops and restaurants can be found lining the main road.

## BEACHES

The Themis Beach Hotel at the eastern end of the resort has cornered the biggest and most sheltered stretch of golden sand, but it is open to the public and has plenty of facilities, including a children's play area.

## THINGS TO SEE & DO

### Megaron Nirou

The excavated and partly reconstructed remains of a two-storey Minoan villa dating to the 16th century BC. Many ceremonial vessels were found inside, and it's thought it may have been a high priest's home.
ⓐ On the outskirts of Kokkini Hani, on the Iraklion side ⓒ 08.30–15.00 Tues–Sun, closed Mon

### Water City

The biggest and best water park on the island. Enjoy its 34 watergames, speed down one of its slides, drift along Lazy River, or just enjoy a swim in one of the swimming pools. Full range of snack-bar and restaurant facilities.
ⓐ Inland from Kokkini Hani along the Anopoli road ⓣ 28107 81317
ⓦ www.watercity.gr ⓒ 10.00–18.30 ⓘ Admission charge

### Watersports

Windsurfing and waterskiing are available through the Themis Beach Hotel. ⓐ Eastern end of the beach ⓣ 28107 61412

🔺 *Kokkini Hani's pleasant strip of beach*

## TAKING A BREAK

**Elotia £** Good, average-priced taverna with a full range of Greek dishes. Pretty, covered restaurant with a blackboard menu full of the most popular dishes and specials. ⓐ Main road, near Themis Beach Hotel entrance ❶ 28107 62451 ❻ 11.00–23.30

**Spyridon £** The best bakery café in the region, with fresh bread, pastries and home-made ice cream. Eat in or take away – if you can stand to wait! ⓐ Main road ❶ 28107 63105 ⓦ http://spyridon-patisserie.com ❻ 08.00–24.00

**Hatzis Taverna ££** Located in the village centre, this taverna dates back to 1937. The tables are attractively laid out around a fountain and the locally caught fish is as fresh as can be. ⓐ Main road ❶ 28107 61251 ❻ 09.00–23.00

**Paximadi ££** With seating both in the restaurant and outside on the waterfront, Paximadi serves everything from pizza to great traditional Greek dishes. ⓐ Beach road ❶ 69774 42541 ❻ 11.30–00.30

# Gouves

Small and still developing, the peaceful resort of Gouves (also called Kato Gouves) lies seaward off the main road and is a great place for winding down. There are narrow stretches of beach in bays along the length of the resort, with those to the west often deserted. There's plenty of choice when it comes to shopping, drinking or eating out. Gouves also makes a good base for exploring the other resorts and sights of the northern coast.

## BEACHES

Good sand and sheltered conditions are to be found close to Gouves's two ports of Aphrodite, to the east, and Marina, to the west. The large beach within the former US Air Force Base, at the west end of the resort, is also open to the public. All types of watersports are on offer on Marina beach.

## THINGS TO SEE & DO

### Big Blue Diving School
Daily diving courses and trips for beginners and advanced divers.
ⓐ Aphrodite Hotel, Beach road ❶ 28970 42363

### Cretaquarium
Meet over 2,500 Mediterranean fish and other animals in Crete's best aquarium just west of Gouves.
ⓐ Thalassocosmos complex, former US base ❶ 28103 37788
Ⓦ www.cretaquarium.gr ❶ 09.00–21.00 ❶ Admission charge

### Tourist train
Eight tourist train departures a day link Gouves with Kokkini Hani. Use it to get to your favourite beach or simply to see the surroundings.
❶ 28970 25270 ❶ 10.00–21.00 ❶ Admission charge

## TAKING A BREAK

The restaurants listed here are all along Gouves' main road leading to the beach, or along the waterfront.

**Porto Gouves £** A modern and breezy café and snack bar right next to the Marina Hotel and overlooking the harbour. Well placed for a quick bite or drink between sunbathing and partying. ⓐ Gouves marina ⓘ 28970 41112 ⓛ 08.00–02.00

**Atlantis ££** A family-friendly restaurant with steaks, fresh fish, sports on TV, Internet and a children's corner. ⓐ Beach road ⓘ 28970 42366 ⓛ 09.00–23.00

**Blue Sky ££** A taverna and café halfway along the national road and beach, serving good Greek dishes. Enjoy dinner on the covered terrace. ⓐ Main street ⓘ 28790 42952 ⓛ 09.00–02.00

⬥ *Gouves is a small but developing resort*

# Hersonissos

Once a small fishing village, Hersonissos is now a complex and cosmopolitan resort with the busy old national road running right through the middle. The rocky coastline hides sandy coves big enough to allow sunbathing and a full range of watersports. Inland lie three old villages ripe for exploration: old Hersonissos, Koutouloufari and Piskopiano.

A thriving port from Classical Greek times, Hersonissos now trades in tourism and is busier than ever. A long linear development, it packs most activities into the space between the main road and the beach. Serious shoppers head for the main road and dice with mopeds, scooters and a constant flow of traffic to buy gold or decorated pottery. Quieter shopping is found in the side streets. If you're looking for nightlife on Crete, then Hersonissos is the place to come. There are plenty of bars and clubs, which stay open until the early hours.

## BEACHES

Like the resort itself, the sandy beaches are narrow and occasionally interrupted by rocky outcrops. A near-solid line of bars, tavernas and souvenir shops crowds the seafront, adding to the busy atmosphere of this resort. The beach road bustles even more in the evening and this is the place to sample a cocktail or cool beer before or after taking dinner at one of the many eating places.

### Anissaras

Situated just to the west of Hersonissos, and quieter than its neighbour, Anissaras is an exclusive resort, packed with upmarket hotels and apartments, but its numerous excellent beaches are open to all visitors. This is a good area for watersports: rental equipment and lessons are available from the beachside hut near the Royal Mare hotel, and you can try diving at the well-signposted Coral Diving Center (☎ 28970 23282 🌐 www.coraldiving.gr).

⬦ *Hersonissos is busy and bustling*

## THINGS TO SEE & DO

### Acqua Plus

Giant slides, black holes, hydrotubes and swimming pools provide
watery action all day long for adults, while children enjoy their own
mini-versions. Plenty of facilities in the way of fast food, restaurants and
bars. Either visit for the full day or pay a reduced amount for a half-day
(after 14.30).

ⓐ On the Kasteli road ⓣ 28970 24950 ⓦ www.acquaplus.gr
ⓛ 10.00–19.00 ⓘ Admission charge

### Boat trips

There are a number of companies offering trips to Sissi and Dia.
These depart once a day from the harbour. You can also hop on the
glass-bottom boat *Nemo* (ⓣ 69494 08570) for a trip around the reefs
near Hersonissos, with a swimming stop in pretty St George's Bay.

### Crete Golf Club

Crete's first golf club is an impressive 18-hole park with great views and
excellent facilities, including a bar, restaurant and shop.
ⓐ 7 km (4 miles) south of town ⓣ 28970 26000 ⓦ www.crete-golf.com

### Horse riding

The village of Avdou, 15 km (9 miles) from Hersonissos in the beautiful
Cretan foothills, houses the **Odysseia Stables**, where beginners and
advanced riders can enjoy the landscape on horseback.
ⓐ Avdou 70005 ⓣ 28970 51080 ⓦ www.horseriding.gr

### Inland villages

Not far inland lies another world. The old villages of Hersonissos,
Koutouloufari and Piskopiano offer a glimpse of a more traditional
way of life, although they are adapting to tourism. It is a steady, uphill
walk to the villages, so you should allow about 30 minutes for this. It is
practical to visit the villages all in one loop, and there are plenty of pit
stops for refreshments or a full meal – consider strolling out to one
for a special dinner.

### Kartland

Have a go at go-karting at this large track packed with twists and turns.
There are even two-seater karts with two steering wheels so two can
drive at the same time! ⓐ Main road, next to Star Beach Water Park
ⓣ 28970 25090 ⓛ 11.00–24.00

## Star Beach Water Park

This water park is actually along the beach so you can choose between lazing on the sand, splashing about in the many water-based attractions around the pools, or joining in one of many other activities such as football, diving, body painting, the daily foam party and regular DJ parties. ⓐ Main road, eastern end ⓣ 28970 29351 ⓦ www.starbeach.gr ⓛ 09.00–19.00 ❶ Admission charge for rides and sunbeds

## Tourist train

A train departs from outside Carera Travel on the main road. It takes visitors on a pleasant one-hour journey around the town and into the old villages to the north.

## TAKING A BREAK

**Danaides £** Housed in a 19th-century building that has lots of rustic charm, Danaides serves authentic Cretan dishes from the grill or wood oven. ⓐ Koutouloufari centre ⓣ 28970 23435 ⓛ 12.00–23.00

**Fegari ££** A 10-minute walk from the main road on the way to Piskopiano, this friendly local taverna is known for the Fegari special: a boned leg of lamb cooked with wine and vegetables. The house wine is decanted from two huge wooden barrels sitting next to the till. ⓐ Along the Piskopiano road ⓣ 28970 24624 ⓛ 17.00–24.00

**Inati ££** Specialising in gourmet-style Cretan cuisine accompanied by fine wines and home-made raki, Inati is an elegant taverna and ideal for a special meal. ⓐ Potamies Pediados ⓣ 28970 51078 ⓛ 17.00–23.00

**Myrtios ££** A trip to Old Hersonissos is the perfect antidote to the busy beach resort. Myrtios has great Greek starters, grilled dishes and pizza straight from the wood-burning oven. The square hosts Greek dancing every Monday and Thursday. ⓐ Main square, Old Hersonissos ⓣ 28970 24761 ⓛ 10.30–24.00

**Passage to India ££** Excellent and authentic Indian food served on a quiet terrace by an Indian family. The restaurant is located across the main road from the church. ⓐ Odos Petrakis ⓣ 28970 23776 ⓛ 10.00–23.00

## AFTER DARK

Hersonissos really heats up at night, with countless bars and clubs catering to the thousands of partygoers that descend on the town in summer.

**Camelot Club** Come to this fake castle on the main street to hear thumping house music and meet hundreds of other happy partygoers. ⓐ Odos Agias Paraskevis 10 ⓣ 69443 14867 ⓦ www.camelotclub.gr ⓛ 23.00–05.00

**Matrix Club** Known for its house, hip-hop and electro music sounds, this is a spacious disco venue with a state-of-the-art sound system. ⓐ Odos Eleftheriou Venizelou ⓣ 28970 21103 ⓦ www.matrixclub.gr ⓛ 23.00–05.00

# Stalis

Much quieter than neighbouring Malia or Hersonissos, relaxing Stalis (called Stalida on some maps) is a very pleasant family oriented resort that has developed beside a fine stretch of golden sands. Nothing is lacking in the way of facilities, and there is a wide choice of tavernas and shops. It also offers more in the way of watersports than many larger resorts.

This purpose-built resort has adopted the ancient name of Stalis, disregarding the modern name of Stalida, which is used on maps and in literature. It is a relatively small but developing resort sandwiched between the main Iraklion road and the sea. Life revolves largely around the beach by day and the tavernas and bars by night. The road behind the beach offers the best opportunity for some gentle retail therapy, whether shopping for basic groceries or for some exotic pieces of jewellery.

Walking eastwards along the beach from Stalis very quickly leads you into the busier resort of Malia (see page 61), offering a much wider range of services.

## BEACHES

With acres of golden sand on hand, it is not difficult to find space on the beach. Facilities are good, with sun loungers, parasols and beach showers all available. Families in particular love this beach, where you can always find room to build a sandcastle or two. For real peace and quiet, and plenty of beach to yourself, head westwards along the beach until the beach road runs out.

## THINGS TO SEE & DO

### Lychnostatis Open-Air Museum

This unusual museum aims to give an insight into typical Cretan life, displaying a traditional furnished house, a restored windmill, a classic white church and a shepherd's shelter. You can finish off with a drink at the bar: try *kanellada* (cinnamon) or *soumada* (almond).

ⓐ Between Stalis and Hersonissos ❶ 28970 23660
ⓦ www.lychnostatis.gr ❶ 09.00–14.00 Sun–Fri, closed Sat
❶ Admission charge

## Watersports

Hang in the air, charge around at high speed or lazily paddle a tiny corner of the Aegean Sea – whatever your fancy, these are all available from the four watersports operators located on the beach near the resort centre. **Slalom** and **Zervas** have the usual range of waterskiing, pedalos and canoes, while **Skyride** and **Seawolf** specialise in more extreme sports like Flying Fish or parasailing. Zervas (❶ 28970 32719 ⓦ www.zervasbeach.com) also has a bar, pool, sunbeds and showers available for guests. Remember to check whether your insurance covers you before taking to the sea or air.

## TAKING A BREAK

Most restaurants can be found along Aghios Ioannis, the street running along the beach.

**Capricciosa £** An extensive menu, from Greek to Italian, and a good menu for children. Generous portions ensure that many guests return.
ⓐ Aghios Ioannis ❶ 28970 31602 ❶ 10.00–24.00

**Amici ££** A lovely family restaurant serving tasty pizzas, steaks and Italian specialities. ⓐ Aghios Ioannis 121, behind the church ❶ 28970 29715
❶ 18.00–01.00

**Maria's Golden Beach ££** Great food and entertainment can be had in this large, open-air restaurant. Besides eating good Greek food, there's Greek dancing with plate-smashing every night. ⓐ Aghios Ioannis
❶ 28970 33240 ❶ 09.00–01.00

🔺 *By day, Stalis life revolves largely around the beach*

**Mythos ££** This is considered one of the best eateries in Stalis, with an extensive menu including pizzas, pasta dishes, mixed grills and a range of Greek favourites. Choose a table on the beach and watch the sun set while you eat. ⓐ Aghios Ioannis ⏰ 09.00–23.00

## AFTER DARK

Although Stalis has some good bars, most people looking for a party head for neighbouring Malia for its throbbing nightlife.

**Akti** A fine beach bar nicely sandwiched between the action along the road and the relaxation on the beach. During the day you can have breakfast and snacks, but it really heats up at night when a happy crowd comes to sip cocktails. ⓐ Aghios Ioannis ⓘ 28970 32167 ⓦ www.crete-web.gr ⏰ 09.00–03.00

**Irish House Pub** An air-conditioned Irish pub with sea view, quiz and karaoke nights, four large screens for sports, live music, DJs and pub food served until 19.00. ⓐ Down an alley at the eastern end of Aghios Ioannis ⓘ 28970 33662 ⏰ 09.00–04.00

● *Stalis caters for the energetic and the not-so-energetic*

# Malia

Busy, hectic, lively, noisy Malia is a resort for all occasions, especially for those who live life 24 hours a day. Families might prefer the peace and quiet found away from the centre, still close enough to enjoy all the facilities of the resort, including the magnificent beaches. The adjacent old village provides a touch of traditional atmosphere.

Seaward of the old national road lies the modern resort, where all activities are focused. As you stroll down the road towards the beach, past the shops, fast-food outlets and bars, the resort seems lively enough by day – but it really only comes to life after sundown. Then it throbs the night away to the beat of loud music from the various bars and, because all that dancing is bound to make you peckish, the fast-food joints stay open all night. Inland from here lies the old village, offering a very different atmosphere. This is the home of the more traditional tavernas, which are tucked away in its maze of twisting, winding streets.

## BEACHES

Malia is not short of sand, and there are huge beaches stretching away eastwards. Families might prefer to use the beach facilities at the Sun Beach Hotel, which has a small children's play area. Those looking for well-organised facilities, with showers, sunbed rental and bars immediately to hand, should head for the central section, but quieter stretches of beach are found by walking out eastwards to Tropical Beach just past the port, where you can escape the crowds and the music. Sandy Beach, best reached from the Malia Palace road, has a beach bar and lots of space.

## THINGS TO SEE & DO

### Boat trip

For a relaxing alternative, board the *Argo* for a day of fun on and around Dia Island. There's a barbecue lunch, two long stops for swimming and

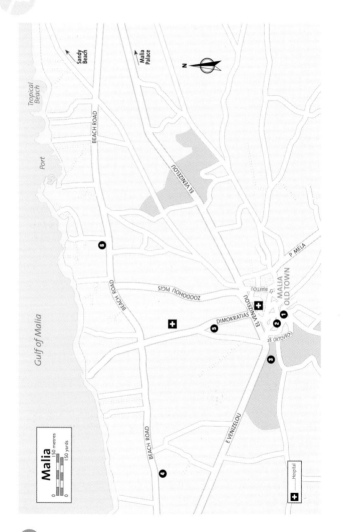

watersports, and you can walk around Panagia Bay on the island.
ⓐ Malia harbour 🕒 Departs 09.30 ❶ Admission charge

## Live Greek music

Try one of the tavernas in the square in Malia old town for a meal to the sound of live Greek music. Arrive about 19.30 to be sure of a table.

## Malia Palace

On the eastern outskirts of Malia lies a remarkable and extensive Minoan palace. In many ways it is more evocative than Knossos, since little or no reconstruction has been attempted – what you see is what the Minoans left behind. Many of the finds are in the Iraklion **Archaeological Museum** (see page 43). There is good information on-site, and plenty to see – including archaeologists at work, since excavations are still continuing. The latest discoveries are being made in a covered area west of the main site, as archaeologists uncover remains of a considerable town that surrounded the palace.
ⓐ East of Malia near the beach, within cycling distance 🕒 08.00–20.00 (summer); 08.30–15.00 (winter) ❶ Admission charge

## Watersports

**Sea Waves Sports**, on the main Malia beach, offers waterskiing, pedalos and more.

## TAKING A BREAK

Head into Malia's old village for relatively traditional eating in a quieter atmosphere, and to Dimokratias Street leading to the beach for variety and more competitive prices.

**Kalesma ££** ❶ No main dishes, only *mezedes* (typical Greek titbits, like Spanish tapas). You'll need about five to six dishes for two people.
ⓐ Omirou 8, Malia old town ☎ 28970 33125 Ⓦ www.kalesma.gr
🕒 11.00–24.00

⬤ *One of Malia's huge beaches*

**Odas ££** ❷ Enjoy dining in the roof garden of this restaurant, which serves a varied menu and is located in a quiet part of the old town. ⓐ Plateia Aghios Yiannis, Malia old town ❶ 28970 33257 ◗ 18.00–24.00

**Soda Bar ££** ❸ A fun, chilled-out café and lounge bar beside the church. Popular with young Brits for the relaxed atmosphere as well as for its great steaks, pizza and pasta. ⓐ E Venizelou 120 ❶ 28970 31577 ◗ 08.00–01.00

## AFTER DARK

**Banana Club** ❹ New to Malia, this popular club is fast becoming one of Crete's top venues for R&B, electro and indie sounds. ⓐ Odos Malia (Beach Road) Ⓦ www.bananaclub.gr

**The Factory** ❺ A nightclub playing a variety of music including electro and R&B. ⓐ Dimokratias ◗ 22.00–05.00

**Zig Zag** ❻ Enjoy cocktails and loud trance and house music. ⓐ Odos Malia (Beach Road) ❶ 28103 43344 Ⓦ www.zigzagclub.gr

# Aghios Nikolaos

The lake and the life that surrounds it are the big attractions of this picturesque town lying in the Gulf of Mirambelou. The capital of the Lasithi province, 'Ag Nik', as tourists like to call it, is an easy-going paradise for those wishing to relax. Little now remains of its past – there are no traces of the ancient city of Lato Etera or the fact that the Venetians built a fortress here. Tourists discovered this town in the 1960s and since then the harbour has attracted an international audience.

The lake is joined to the sea by a narrow canal; views from the hill overlooking this are quite breathtaking. The high cliffs, lush green vegetation, colourful fishing boats and tranquil restaurants make the lake an ideal place to come either at night or during the day.

A British naval traveller named Spratt measured the depth of the lake and discovered that it was over 64 m (200 ft) deep. This led him to believe that it was the opening of a deep river, and this is most probably the reason why it has become known as the 'bottomless lake'. In 1867 a canal was made between the lake and the sea, helping to keep the blue waters crystal clear.

## BEACHES

Aghios Nikolaos is proud to be the municipality with the most blue-flag beaches in Greece – it has no fewer than 23 of them.

There are numerous beaches surrounding the port. The closest are **Ammos** and **Kitroplatia**, which are not particularly stunning but worth a few hours' sunbathing. Both have good facilities. A little further south, but worth the trip, is **Almyros**, an aquatic national reserve due to its unusual vegetation of cane bulrushes, tall trees and rare species of bird. A cool spring trickles into the sea. The beach is well organised and the water is shallow, ideal for families. More beaches lie to the north of the town, some immaculate and surrounded by upmarket hotels with private pools.

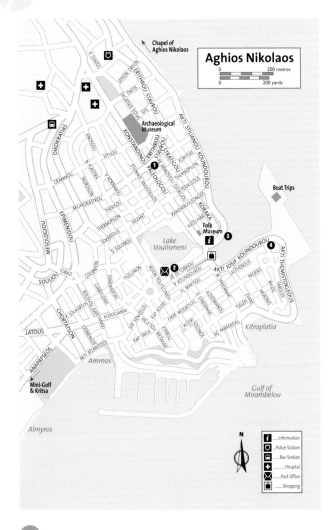

Aghios Nikolaos

Chapel of Aghios Nikolaos

0    200 metres
0    200 yards

Boat Trips

Archaeological Museum

Lake Voulismeni

Folk Museum

Mini-Golf & Kritsa

Ammos

Kitroplatia

Gulf of Mirambelou

Almyros

N

i ......Information
......Police Station
......Bus Station
......Hospital
......Post Office
......Shopping

## THINGS TO SEE & DO

### Archaeological Museum

A short walk uphill from the lake, this is a modern, well-thought out attraction with some interesting artefacts. It has pre- and early Minoan finds and an impressive vase in the shape of the Goddess of Mirtos. There is also an assortment of painted clay coffins and bathtubs, and the grinning skull of a Roman, his forehead encircled with gold olive leaves.
ⓐ Odos Konstandinou Paleologou 74 ⓘ 28410 24943 ⓒ 08.30–15.00 Tues–Sun, closed Mon ⓘ Admission charge

### Boat trips

There are short trips from the harbour to the island of Spinalonga (although boats to Spinalonga leave more frequently from Elounda or Plaka). **Nostos Tours** organises regular fishing trips, and there are also occasional boat excursions to other islands, Mohlos village and coastal cruises. For something different, board the **Nautilos** 'submarine' boat with its large underwater windows for a short tour of the underwater world near town. The tourist information office has more details.
ⓘ 28410 22357 ⓒ Departs four times between 11.00 and 15.30

### Folk Museum

A small but interesting collection of handicrafts, costumes, utensils and everyday Cretan artefacts.
ⓐ Odos Konstandinou Paleologou, next to the tourist office
ⓒ 10.30–16.30, 18.00–20.00 Mon–Sat, closed Sun ⓘ Admission charge

> **SHOPPING**
> Aghios Nikolaos has some of Crete's best shopping, with quality boutiques in the streets that run up from the harbour – Odos 28 Octobriou, Odos Roussou Koundourou and Odos Sfakianaki. Look for antique and modern jewellery, embroidered Cretan blouses and waistcoats, and contemporary crafts.

### Mini-Golf

All the family will enjoy this place. As well as golf it offers table tennis,
a children's pool, playground, restaurants and bars.
ⓐ Opposite the Municipal beach club to the south of town
ⓛ 09.00–23.00 ❶ Admission charge

### EXCURSIONS

To see the **Chapel of Aghios Nikolaos**, which the town was named after,
drive north of town, following signs off the coast road to the right,
heading towards the sea. For a pretty village with lovely craft shops, drive
9 km (6 miles) west of Aghios Nikolaos to **Kritsa**.

### TAKING A BREAK

**Aovas £ ❶**   Set back slightly from the road, this is a good place to go
for traditional Greek food. Try the stuffed vine leaves or rabbit stifado.
ⓐ Odos Konstandinou Paleologou 44 ❶ 28410 23231 ⓛ 10.00–late

**Peripou £ ❷**   A book and CD shop and Internet café with great coffee
and snacks. ⓐ Odos 28 Octobriou 25 ❶ 28410 24876 ⓛ 09.30–03.00

### AFTER DARK

**Armida ❸**   The former cargo ship's lightly swaying deck is the perfect
place to catch the evening breeze and enjoy a cocktail. ⓐ Docked near
the tourist office ❶ 69479 92577 ⓛ 10.00–03.00

**Molo ❹**   A beautifully designed café-bar overlooking the harbour
where all the elegant people meet at night. Molo serves light breakfasts,
lunch and dinner, and then turns into a lounge club with regular parties.
ⓐ Akti Iosif Koundourou 6 ❶ 28410 26250 ⓦ www.molo.gr
ⓛ 08.30–04.00

❶ *One of Crete's many idyllic beaches*

# EXCURSIONS
Out & about

◓ *The magnificent Samaria Gorge*

# The Samaria Gorge

A national park since 1962, the Samaria Gorge is one of the great natural wonders of Europe. Thousands of visitors walk it every year. This is not done without some toil, but the sense of achievement and satisfaction is immeasurable. For those not wishing to walk the full length, an easier option allows access as far as the great 'Iron Gates'.

The Samaria Gorge usually opens for walkers in May, once the river has subsided sufficiently to allow for safe walking; it closes in October, at the approach of the rainy season. Precise dates depend on weather conditions. Starting high on the Omalos Plain, at an altitude of around 1,220 m (4,000 ft), the walk is around 15 km (9¹/₂ miles) in length. Most of this is downhill, only levelling out at the approach to Aghia Roumeli, at the coast. Allow between five and seven hours for the walk, depending on the conditions.

The gorge is a national park and rules do apply: no camping, no fires, no smoking, no alcohol and certainly no interfering with the wildlife and flora. If you respect these rules, you will have no problems with the helpful wardens that patrol the park.

## TRANSPORT

Although it is possible to do this walk using public transport or taxis, an organised trip is the best option, especially since an experienced guide accompanies the tour. Transport is laid on (with a very early start) to take you to the start of the gorge. Breakfast can be taken either at Omalos village or at Xyloskalo, the hamlet at the entrance to the gorge. The walk ends at Aghia Roumeli on the Libyan Sea. From there, a ferry transports walkers along the coast to Hora Sfakion, where coaches await you for the return journey.

## PREPARATIONS

Walking the Samaria Gorge is not something that can be undertaken lightly. Downhill it may be, but it can still be very tiring. Sensible preparations and precautions can do much to ensure a successful day.

**Footwear** Sensible shoes are key. Good, strong trainers are required, at the very least; walking shoes or boots are much preferred. Be warned – walkers with inadequate footwear may not be allowed to enter.

**Sun protection** Not all of the gorge enjoys shade, so it is important to guard against the sun and keep suncream handy. A hat is essential.

**Water** It is important to carry a bottle of water – at least a litre per person. There are springs for drinking water at various stages down the gorge. The last water in the gorge is just before entering the narrowest section. There are toilets and rest stations at various points.

**Your guide** Route finding is no problem – the path is easily followed. The function of the guide is to keep an eye on the party. Usually, the guide takes a longer breakfast and gives his party a head start. Following behind means that help can be offered to anyone lagging behind or in any difficulty. Guides can also summon the rescue services, if necessary.

## THINGS TO SEE & DO

### Xyloskalo – the head of the gorge

Wooden steps, from which the name of the hamlet of Xyloskalo is derived, lead down from the entrance into the gorge itself. Pine trees provide some shade on this steep and steady descent, and the rock face of Gingilos provides a dramatic alpine backdrop. Eventually, towards the bottom of the gorge, the path joins the Tarraios River, which runs through the gorge to the sea at Aghia Roumeli. Although it is usually dry at the higher end of the gorge, lower down the river flows for most of the summer.

### Samaria Village

The old village of Samaria is met roughly halfway through. Its remaining inhabitants were moved out when the area was declared a national park

**THE LAZY WAY**
For this option, visitors are taken by coach to Hora Sfakion and by ferry to Aghia Roumeli. A 2-km (1¼-mile) walk, slightly uphill, leads to the entrance of the gorge. A further walk soon leads to the narrowest and most spectacular part of the gorge. The lazy way it might be, but this is no soft option. The route is fully exposed to the sun, and forms the hottest part of the walk. Water must be carried and sensible footwear is essential.

in 1962. It makes a good resting place, and is where most walkers stop for a picnic. *Kri-kri* (wild goats) still survive within the gorge, and it is not unusual to see them in and around the old village.

### Iron Gates

The scenery around here rarely lacks drama but, from here on down, the gorge steadily closes in until there is only room for the river, with the cliffs rising vertically above. This spot is called Sideroportes (Iron Gates), and it is hard to imagine a more fitting climax to this spectacular walk.

### Aghia Roumeli

Refreshments are available immediately on passing through the exit gate, and Aghia Roumeli is just 2 km (1¼ miles) away. After the dryness of the gorge, Aghia Roumeli seems an absolute oasis, with tavernas, shops and accommodation. There is a small beach for a refreshing paddle or swim after the walk.

# Gortys, Faistos & Aghia Triada

It is worth hiring a car to drive south, through ever-changing countryside, to visit some of the most important archaeological sites on Crete. Starting from Iraklion, this 150-km (93-mile) day trip takes in the Roman city of Gortina, now called Gortys, the remains of which lie scattered among olive trees, plus the Minoan palaces of Faistos and Aghia Triada, sitting in the tranquil mountains. There is the opportunity to have lunch or relax on the beach at Matala (see page 37) , or even stay for one of its reputedly fantastic sunsets.

All these sites can just as easily be reached from Rethymnon, along the Spili to Mires road. From Iraklion follow signs to Mires, and head south via Agii Deka. Look for the site entrance to the right on reaching Gortys.

## GORTYS

The remains of this one-time capital of Roman Crete lie scattered over a large area, among the surrounding olive groves and on the hillside above the site. A café and display of statues are found to the right of the entrance and the entry charge gives access to the fenced-off area around the Church of Aghios Titos. St Titos was sent by St Paul to convert Crete to Christianity and became the first Bishop of Crete. Also in this enclosure is the Roman agora (marketplace), an odeon (small theatre) and long wall on which the Laws of Gortina are written in Ancient Greek. ☎ 28920 31144
🕐 08.00–20.00 (summer); 08.30–15.00 (winter)
❶ Admission charge

## FAISTOS

Continue past Mires, and look for the signposted left turn to Faistos. Set on a hilltop, the **Minoan palace of Faistos** provides a marvellous panorama over the surrounding countryside. Smaller than Knossos, but in many ways similar to it, this palace was rebuilt after earthquake damage. Most of what is seen now is the New Palace, the older part being to the left of the site entrance. This older part is where the original Minoan town once spread down to the plain below.

◯ *Some of the many remains of Roman Crete at Gortys*

🕿 28920 42315  🕒 08.00–20.00 (summer); 08.30–15.00 (winter)
ⓘ Admission charge

## AGHIA TRIADA

To reach Aghia Triada, continue past the car park and take the
right-forking road almost immediately. This elevated road offers superb
views over the plain as it winds along the hillside for 3 km (2 miles)
until the surfaced road ends at the car park. The Minoan villa and small
town lie in a wonderful pastoral setting overlooking the Mesara Gulf.
In Minoan times, the plain below was probably covered by the sea, which
would have lapped the base of the hill. This evocative site was once
thought to have been an extension to the palace at Faistos, used as
a summer residence and known as the Royal Villa. Later finds and the
existence of a small town cast doubts on that purpose, suggesting
either a cult association or a central gathering point for celebrations.
🕿 28102 26470  🕒 08.00–20.00 (summer); 08.30–15.00 (winter)
ⓘ Admission charge

⬥ The panoramic view from the Minoan palace at Faistos

# Knossos

Knossos offers a fascinating backward glance over 4,000 years, to the earliest known organised civilisation in the Mediterranean. Not only does Knossos qualify as one of the world's most important archaeological sites, but also it is one of the most visited. Most of the vast treasures and finds from the site are housed in Iraklion's **Archaeological Museum** (see page 43).

## GETTING THERE

The site of ancient Knossos is located some 5 km (3 miles) from the centre of Iraklion, and is best reached from the city on bus No 2. If you're driving, ask for detailed directions as the typically Greek signposting is very bad. It can get very busy, so try to visit the site very early or late in the afternoon to avoid the main crush of visitors between 10.00 and 15.00. Joining a guided tour from nearly any resort on Crete will greatly enhance your understanding of the site. Guides are also available at Knossos, but be careful to use an official one and agree on the price beforehand. Alternatively, buy a guidebook and enjoy the site at your own pace. ❶ 28102 31940 ❷ 08.00–20.00 (summer); 08.30–15.00 (winter) ❶ Admission charge

## BACKGROUND

Evidence suggests that the earliest settlement on this site was Neolithic (from around 6000 BC). The Minoans arrived around 3500 BC, bringing skills in bronze working, and they survived until around 1100 BC. Their civilisation is often divided into Early, Middle and Late periods, and these too are usually subdivided. Interest really starts in the Middle Minoan period, around 2000 BC, when the first palaces were built, encouraging a more centralised society. These early palaces were destroyed by earthquakes around 1700 BC (marking the start of the Late Minoan period) but they were rebuilt in a more elaborate style. It is the remains of these last palaces that are visible today.

## DISCOVERY

Arthur Evans began digging at Knossos in 1900 and was soon making spectacular finds that astonished the whole of Europe. Without the scientific backing of present-day knowledge, Evans' interpretation and theories were on the whole remarkably accurate, although many are challenged in detail today.

> ### MYTH OF THE MINOTAUR
> The complex underground network of corridors and rooms in this Minoan palace gave rise to the myth of the Minotaur. According to legend, this bull-headed monster was kept in a labyrinth and fed on human flesh.

## SITE TOUR

There is much to see and understand in this ancient palace. The following account concentrates on the main features and is, by necessity, brief. Organised trips usually combine Knossos with a trip to the museum in Iraklion (see page 43), where many of the finds are housed.

**West Court** This is the first part reached from the entrance. Notice here three large pits which are thought to have been repositories for offertory oil, wine and sacrificial animals. The court runs up to the West Façade, which is faced with gypsum blocks, now badly weathered. Quarried locally, the gypsum cladding made the palace appear gleaming white. Following around to the right leads to the West Porch and excavated remains of later houses.

**Corridor of the Procession Fresco** From the porch, wooden doors opened to this corridor. The walls on both sides were lined with huge frescoes showing figures in procession. Landslip has destroyed much of the corridor.

**South Propylea** This paved area is especially visited to see a copy of the Cup Bearer Fresco, one of the best-preserved parts of the fresco from the

⬢ *Knossos: 4,000 years of history*

⬤ *One of the reconstructed frescoes at Knossos*

corridor. Red supporting columns were used in the reconstruction. These were once wooden, often whole trees with the thicker ends uppermost. From here a staircase leads to the main reception rooms. Storerooms full of *pithoi* (giant storage jars) – used for grain, oil and wine – are still in place and can be seen from the upper long corridor. Reproductions of some of the most famous frescoes lie in this area.

**Central Court**  This large, open space gives access to the throne room on the right. Remarkably, the original gypsum throne, in the inner sanctum, now some 3,500 years old, survives intact.

**Royal Apartments**  These lie on the opposite side of the Central Court and include the Grand Staircase, the Queen's Megaron (Central Hall), complete with bathroom, and the Hall of the Double Axes (the King's Megaron).

**The Charging Bull**  Leaving the Central Court by the north entrance brings you face to face with the relief of the Charging Bull, the original of which is now in the museum in Iraklion.

# The Lasithi Plateau

With its white-sailed windmills, the Lasithi Plateau is one of the abiding images of Crete. There are not so many windmills today, but this fertile plateau still rumbles on with a donkey-driven rural lifestyle. Tourists provide a new outlet for the traditional handicrafts, lace and woven carpets, which often decorate the roadsides. From the highway at Malia, this day trip is about 120 km (75 miles).

From the highway, follow the signs to Mochos and the Lasithi Plateau. Follow the road as it winds upwards to 800 m (2,600 ft) and dramatically arrives at the Lasithi Plateau through a cutting lined with the relics of stone windmills once used for grinding grain.

The Lasithi Plateau, a patchwork of green fields, flanked by the stark slopes of the Dikti Mountains, is extremely fertile and grows a wide range of vegetables, grain and fruit, though frequent winter snow makes it unsuitable for olives or citrus crops. The white-sailed windpumps are a product of 15th-century Venetian engineering. There were 10,000 windmills at one time. Far fewer operate now, although many of their skeletons still stand. A windmill in full sail these days usually signifies a taverna.

Turn right at the first junction to pass through Kato Metochi and Plati, with its tempting displays of craftwork hung along the street. Turn right on entering Psikro.

## THINGS TO SEE & DO

### The Diktean Cave

According to legend, this cave is the birthplace of the god Zeus. His father, Kronos, fearing that a son would usurp his power, had sworn to eat any male offspring. Rea, the wife of Kronos, tricked her husband by giving him a stone to eat while leaving Zeus hidden in this cave. The baby was protected by the Kouretes, who beat their shields outside to disguise the baby's cries. Follow the road flanked by carpets to reach the car park. You can hire a donkey (at great expense) to ride up to the

cave entrance, or climb steadily 105 m (345 ft) to the top. After entering the moderately illuminated cave, follow the steps deep down into its interior for views of the stalactites and stalagmites. The game now is to spot the stone nipples where young Zeus was suckled. The smooth steps leading up to the Diktean Cave are very slippery, so make sure you wear proper footwear. It can get quite cold, so take a jumper. 🕐 08.00–18.30 (summer) ❶ Admission charge

### Cretan museums & windmills

Pretty villages follow in succession as the tour around the plateau continues. Aghios Georgios is worth a stop for its folk museum. Located in a typical village house, it gives an insight into the old Cretan way of life. Furnished rooms, tools, costumes and farming implements are all well displayed in a series of rooms. 🕐 10.00–17.00 ❶ Small admission charge

Just up the road in Aghios Georgios is a small museum dedicated to Eleftherios Venizelos, displaying photos, documents and objects relating to Crete's most famous statesman. The staff will be happy to explain why he is so important for Crete.

There are one or two working windmills to see on the last part of the drive around the plateau, as well as the largest town, Tzermiado. This is the last chance to buy a carpet or lacework before leaving the plateau. Leave the plateau once you have passed through Pinakiano.

### A BITE TO EAT

**Kali Mera £** This pretty restaurant, 1.5 km (less than a mile) before the village of Psikro, is a great spot for lunch. It has inspiring views over the plateau with the huge mountain range in the background framing the landscape. The restaurant is covered in flowers. The food is simple and very Greek. ⓐ Aghios Charalampos ☎ 28440 31913 🕐 07.00–late

# Santorini

Unique among Greek islands, Santorini is the stuff of picture postcards, a visual experience not to be missed. Cube-shaped white houses nestle tightly on dark, volcanic hillsides to create memorable images. Organised day trips from Crete allow visitors to see the capital, Fira, and explore other parts of the island and the caldera (crater), making for a long but satisfying day out. In fact, a day is not long enough for many visitors and if you have time it's easy to arrange a longer trip to Santorini.

Explosive volcanic activity here, particularly around 1450 BC, is believed to have contributed to the decline of the Minoan civilisation on Crete, creating such upheavals that this once-circular island was left shredded in fragments. Thira is the name of the largest of the islands left in the aftermath.

## BEACHES

Because of its volcanic history, Santorini is renowned for its many coloured beaches. You can choose from secluded areas to the more cosmopolitan, with watersports and a range of facilities. Here are the main beaches.

**Akrotiri**  This is the famous red beach of the island near the Church of Aghios Nikolaos.

**Avis**  This can be found in between the resorts of Kamari and Monolithos and is very good for watersports.

**Kamari**  A large, well-known beach with all the facilities you could ever want or need.

**Monolithos**  A popular beach with shallow waters.

**Oia**  The port of Armeni, below the town of Oia, has many small areas for swimming and sunbathing. Close by are also the beaches of Baxedes and Kouloumbos.

**Perivolos**  This is the longest beach on the island, stretching from Perissa village to Perivolos. It is possibly also the most popular because of its many tavernas, bars and various watersports.

○ *Kick back and relax on Vlichada Beach*

**Vlichada** Right down on the southernmost point of the island, this beach is unique because of its sand dunes, which have often been likened to a lunar landscape.

### GETTING THERE

Large, slow cruise ships and more expensive but much faster catamaran ferries offer day cruises from Iraklion. The cruise ships depart very early, as they take four hours to get to Santorini, whereas the catamaran takes just two hours. The cruise ships, however, often have additional facilities such as swimming pools and restaurants, and offer great views as you sail into port. Ferries run out of Aghios Nikolaos and Sitia too.

### THE CRUISE

On organised cruise trips, you'll board around 06.30, have breakfast on board, and get information about the island and the tour options you can book. After arrival at about 11.30, passengers booked on tours are let off first at the main harbour, after which the remaining passengers are sailed to Fira's small harbour for the cable car or donkey ride to the town.

Excursions include:

**A beach day at Pyrgos or Kamari** (see pages 87 and 90) Laze the hottest part of the day away on Santorini's famous black sands before heading back to town for dinner and sunset.

**Hot springs & volcano** A small boat sails out to two of the islets within the group to explore the hot springs on Palea Kameni and then the sulphurous volcano on Nea Kameni.

**Round the island tour** This visits Pyrgos (see page 87) and Oia (see page 92) before returning to the capital, Fira. Oia is the longest stop, allowing time for lunch to be taken in one of the many tavernas.

If you'd like to arrange your own tour of the island, contact Kamari Tours (☎ 22860 31390 Ⓦ www.kamaritours.gr) before departure.

## THINGS TO SEE & DO

### Akrotiri

The famous prehistoric settlement of Akrotiri is at the southern end of the island. The ruins of this well-developed Minoan-type civilisation date from the late Bronze Age (1650–1500 BC) and have survived well due to the layer of ash that preserved the town after the great eruption of the Thira volcano. This catastrophe submerged much of the island, and the resulting clouds of ash and tidal waves probably wiped out Minoan civilisation on Crete too. Thira has also often been seen as the mythical lost city of Atlantis. The three-storey houses found here may have been the first high-rise buildings in history. The wall paintings are the earliest example of large-scale painting in Europe. The site is currently being prepared to handle more visitors and is expected to reopen from 2011, but excellent exhibitions on the town can be seen in the archaeological museum (see page 89) and at the wall-paintings exhibition (see page 89) in Fira.

Ⓐ Akrotiri Archaeological Museum ☎ 22860 81366 ⏱ 08.30–15.00
Tues- Sun, closed Mon ❶ Admission charge

## Boat tours

Hop on the *Nissos* for an all-day tour of the caldera, stopping off at the
volcano, hot springs on Thirassia island and Oia. Alternatively, you can
book the *Anemos* (☎ 22860 22932) for sightseeing, fishing or swimming
trips, often at better prices than the organised tours.

## Pyrgos

The old capital, Pyrgos, is an attractive fortified town dating back to the
Middle Ages and offers great views from the castle at the highest point.
There are several cafés and snack bars around for those not choosing to
walk up.

## Winery tour

There are 840 vine growers on the island, harvesting 2,540 hectares
(6,276 acres) of land. Several wineries can be visited, but the **SantoWines
Oenotourism Center** is arguably the nicest, located 4 km (2¹/₂ miles)
south of Fira. Not only is it one of the largest producers on the island, but

### WINEMAKING ON SANTORINI

Santorini's unique climate of very hot, dry conditions and harsh
winds means that the growers have had to invent a way of
training and pruning the vines that they call *koulooura* (curl).
The vines are pruned into the shape of a basket and, for their
protection, the grapes are placed in the centre. The night mists
provide moisture for the vine, and the volcanic earth the variety of
minerals that help the grapes to flourish. Of the well-known
wines, the Nikteri and Vinsanto are the most famous. The latter is
a sweet red wine made from grapes that have been dried in the
sun for 10 to 15 days.

it's perched right on the caldera rim and the views from here are even better when you're tipsy (though mind the drop). Visitors can do a tour of the modern plant and sample a few of their excellent vintages.
📞 22860 22596 🌐 www.santowines.gr 🕐 09.30–21.00 Mon–Sat, closed Sun ❶ Admission charge for tours

## FIRA (THIRA)

Situated around the hilltop on several terraces, Fira boasts white houses, pretty churches, narrow streets, cafés, restaurants, fast-food outlets and tourist shops. Bargain hunters can spend their day haggling for gold, silver, Cretan fashions or onyx chess sets. The best things are free, however, and that includes the magnificent views

🔺 The central bay of Santorini

from the cliffs. Every 20 minutes, a cable car links the town to the harbour below.

## THINGS TO SEE & DO

### Museum of Prehistoric Thira

An excellent archaeological museum displaying finds from Akrotiri and highlighting different aspects of life in this prehistoric town. Unusually for Greece there are good accompanying English texts.

ⓐ South of town, near the bus station ☎ 22860 23077 🕒 10.00–16.00 Mon–Sat (summer); 08.30–15.00 Mon–Sat (winter), closed Sun

### Thira Foundation

For those fascinated by Santorini's ancient history, this exhibition has 3D, life-size reproductions of Akrotiri's magnificent wall paintings, decorated with people, monkeys, insects and dolphins.

ⓐ 200 m (219 yds) north of the cable-car station ☎ 22860 23016
ⓦ www.therafoundation.org 🕒 10.00–16.00 Mon–Sat, closed Sun

## TAKING A BREAK

**Naoussa ££** A lovely taverna in the centre of Fira serving fresh fish, mussels, moussaka and stuffed vegetables. The top floor has great views of the caldera. ⓐ Main street ☎ 22860 24869
ⓦ www.naoussa-restaurant.gr 🕒 10.00–23.00

**Nicolas ££** Traditional Greek cuisine with a blackboard menu that changes every day. The menu is in Greek but the owners will happily translate everything for you. ⓐ Main street ☎ 22860 24550
🕒 12.00–15.00, 18.00–24.00

**Stani ££** A popular restaurant in the bustling shopping streets of Fira. A staircase leads up to the roof from where you have good caldera views.
ⓐ Main street, near the cable car ☎ 22860 23078 🕒 10.00–24.00

## KAMARI

A bustling but pleasant low-rise resort on the eastern coast, the modern resort of Kamari stretches along a pebbly black beach with a mountain dramatically rising from the sea nearby.

## THINGS TO SEE & DO

### 3S Watersports

A wide range of watersports including waterskiing, windsurfing, sailing, banana boats and ringos.

ⓐ Kamari beach ⓣ 69327 80852 ⓦ www.3sxsport.gr ⓛ 09.30–19.00

### Kamari cinema

The outdoor cinema on the western outskirts of Kamari is a fun way to see a film. Food and drink can be bought from the bar at the back, before the film or at the half-time interval. Films are in the original language with Greek subtitles.

ⓣ 22860 31974 ⓦ www.cinekamari.gr ⓛ Screenings start at 21.30

### Mountain biking

**Motor Inn** hires out good-quality bikes and organises bike trips.

ⓣ 22860 31165 ⓦ www.motorinn.gr ⓛ 08.00–24.00

### Navy's Dive Centre

A well-organised five-star PADI dive centre next to the beach with its own café and restaurant. You can do anything from beginners' trial dives to instructor courses.

ⓐ Beach road ⓣ 22860 31033 ⓦ www.navys.gr

## TAKING A BREAK

**Atmosphere £££** Fine international cuisine in stylish surroundings within earshot of waves crashing on the beach. ⓐ Beach promenade
ⓣ 22860 31368 ⓦ www.atmosphere-restaurant.gr ⓛ 18.00–23.00

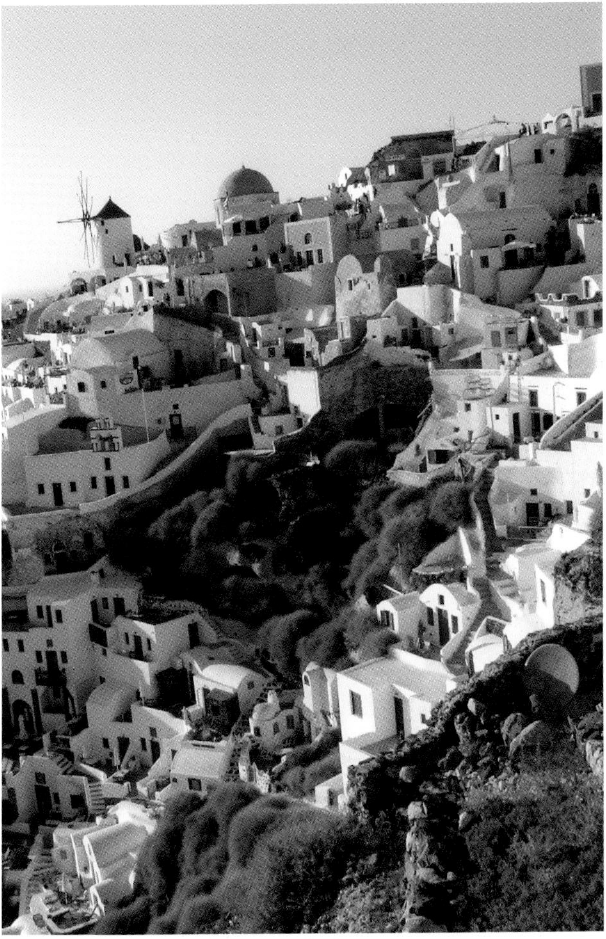

Oia's picture-perfect cluster of white houses

## OIA

Located in the north of the island, the fishing village of Oia (pronounced 'Eea') was severely damaged by an earthquake in 1956 but has been rebuilt in traditional Cycladic style. With its clustered white houses, tiny courtyards, colourful churches and narrow streets, it competes strongly for the title of prettiest village on the island. Oia is the place where artists gather, their work inspired by the magnificent surroundings. Thousands of people head here every evening to watch the sunset.

## THINGS TO SEE & DO

### Armeni

This small traditional port is the harbour of Oia, best reached via the steep, winding steps. There are a few tavernas here, but most people make the trip for a refreshing swim in the clear water.

## TAKING A BREAK

**Melenio £** A wonderful café and patisserie with a display filled with delicious cakes, pastries and snacks. The terrace at the back has views over the caldera. ⓐ Oia, main alley ❶ 22860 71149 ⓛ 09.00–01.00

**Pelekanos ££** A friendly rooftop café and restaurant with stunning views of Oia and the caldera beyond. Light snacks and Greek dishes are served, and there's Internet access too. ❶ 22860 71553 ⓦ www.pelekanosrestaurant.gr ⓛ 11.00–01.00

**1800 £££** This is Santorini's best restaurant, set in a beautiful old captain's house in the heart of Oia. The cuisine is Mediterranean using only fresh ingredients and accompanied by excellent local wines. ⓐ Oia, main alley ❶ 22860 71485 ⓦ www.oia-1800.com ⓛ 20.00–01.00 ❶ Booking ahead essential

❶ *Traditional Cretan fishing boat, laden with sponges and shells*

## LIFESTYLE
Cretan delights

# Food & drink

## GREEK DELIGHTS

Greek cooking uses the freshest ingredients, and is nourishing, tasty and filling. As there are a large number of vegetable dishes, this is a cuisine ideally suited to vegetarians (ask for *horis kreas* – without meat). So, although in every resort you will be sure to come across English standards – like bacon and eggs, chips, shepherd's pie, and roast beef and Yorkshire pudding – do not miss out on what the Greeks have to offer.

## CRETAN DISHES

Venture into a traditional taverna away from tourist areas and you will find a whole range of Cretan specialities, such as *staka* (melted cheese mopped up with bread) or *dakos* (rusk-type bread sprinkled with olive oil, cheese and tomato). Part of the fun is to try something different. Fried snails in a vinegar, tomato and herb sauce are especially delicious.

### Appetisers

A typical Greek meal begins with a basket of fresh bread and a selection of *mezedes* (appetisers). Order several dishes and share them with your friends. Served hot or cold, the highlights are: *horiátiki* – a refreshing salad comprising feta cheese, tomato, cucumber and black olives; *tzatziki* – cucumber and yoghurt dip; *taramasalata* – a paste of cod's roe and lemon juice; and *saganaki* – fried cheese fritter. Cheese or spinach pies also make tasty snacks.

### Main courses

Meat is cheap and plentiful. The most succulent dishes include: *souvlaki* or *shish kebab* – garlic-marinated lamb dressed with onions; *keftedes* – meatballs with mint, onion and eggs; *moussaka* – layers of minced lamb or beef with sliced aubergine and béchamel sauce; and *stifado* – beef with onions and tomato sauce. Or you might like to try *dolmades* – vine-leaf parcels stuffed with rice, minced beef or pork and pine kernels, braised in lemon and olive oil.

🔺 *Saláta horiátiki, a refreshing salad shown here with fried seafood and olives*

Fishermen's catches of red mullet, sole, snapper or sea bream may be brought to your table if you have found a seaside taverna that takes your fancy. Before ordering it is important to remember that fish is sold by weight; negotiate a price first – a good rule of thumb is that 1 kg (2 lb) serves four people.

Prawns, stuffed mussels, fried squid and stewed octopus (often cooked in white wine, with potatoes and tomatoes) are all widely available. Swordfish steaks are popular, but expensive. *Soupia* (cuttlefish) on the barbecue is excellent.

### Snacks

If you are peckish around lunchtime but do not want to sit down to a full meal, *gyros* – doner kebab in pitta bread – or the snack version of *souvlaki* – pitta bread filled with meat, tomato and onion – will fill a hole.

### Desserts

Most Greeks will settle for fresh fruit after a meal – watermelons are unbelievably juicy, or there are apricots, peaches and grapes. If you have a sweet tooth, try *baklava* (a pastry soaked in honey with almonds and walnuts), *loukoumades* (a kind of honey fritter) or *bougatsa* (a hot pie with a creamy filling of custard and cinnamon). More revitalising on a hot day is yoghurt topped with honey and almonds – delicious!

## DRINKS

Soft drinks, like colas and lemonades, are sold everywhere, but freshly made orange or lemon juice is more refreshing in hot weather. Mineral water (still or fizzy) is equally thirst-quenching – Greek brands are perfectly safe and acceptable. Outside the hotels, tea generally means hot water and a tea bag!

Greek coffee is served in small cups, is strong in flavour, has a treacly texture and leaves a thick sediment. Ask for *glyko* if you like it sweet, *metrio* (medium), or *sketo* (without sugar). If you prefer, you can order espresso or instant (ask for *Nes*). And there is nothing more refreshing on a hot day than iced coffee (*frappé*), usually served in a glass and available in packet form (add water!) in supermarkets.

### Spirits

The Greek national drink is *ouzo* (an aniseed-flavoured spirit usually taken as an aperitif). Ouzo can be drunk straight, but if you intend to have more than one glass, follow custom and dilute it with water and ice. You may also be offered *raki* (a spirit made from distilled grape skins and pips). Greek brandy is also highly palatable, and available in various strengths and prices, indicated by star ratings (three, five, seven). The best-known brand of Greek brandy is Metaxa, which is dark and sweet.

## THE *KAFENEION*

In Cretan villages, the *kafeneion* (café) is pivotal to daily life and even the smallest hamlet will have one, probably two. They remain very much a male preserve however, although visitors of both sexes will be made welcome. Traditionally, the *kafeneion* was where workers would go when they took a break from working the fields, or when they had finished for the day. Even today, despite more men working in technology in the towns, they still visit the *kafeneion* at the end of the day. Men come here to read the newspaper, debate the issues of the day and to swap the village gossip. Often it is where they collect their post too. If you happen to pass through a village, look out for men sitting on rickety wooden chairs either in animated conversation or playing *tavli* (backgammon) and consuming *café ellenico* (Greek coffee).

### Wine & beer

The most distinctive Greek wine is *retsina*. Flavoured with resin, it takes some getting used to and you may prefer to drink it with soda water. *Retsina* is a good accompaniment to white fish and is supposed to complement the oil in Greek food.

Crete produces some excellent wines. The island is covered in vineyards and the locals are rightly proud of what they regard as some of the best wines in Greece. There are four main vine-growing areas on the island: Peza, Sitia, Arhanes and Dafnes. Arhanes is thought by some to be the same vineyard that the ancient Minoans cultivated, almost 4,000 years ago.

Greek lager is very drinkable and can be cheaper than imported beer – ask for Mythos or Hellas. The most widely available foreign brands are Heineken, Amstel, Henninger and Budweiser. Specify that you want a bottled or draught beer, as cans are often poor value.

# Menu decoder

Here are some of the authentically Greek dishes that you might encounter in tavernas or pastry shops.

**Dolmades** vine leaves stuffed with rice, onions, parsley, mint, lemon juice and sometimes meat

**Domátes/piperiés yemistés** tomatoes/peppers stuffed with herb-flavoured rice (and sometimes minced pork or beef)

**Fassólia saláta** white beans (haricot, butter beans) dressed with olive oil, lemon juice, parsley, onions, olives and tomato

**Lazánia sto fourno** Greek lasagne, similar to Italian lasagne, but often including additional ingredients, such as chopped boiled egg or sliced, Greek-style sausages

**Makaronópita** pie made from macaroni blended with beaten eggs, cheese and milk, baked in puff pastry

**Melitzanópita** pie made from baked liquidised aubergines mixed with onions, garlic, breadcrumbs, eggs, mint and Parmesan cheese

**Melitzanosaláta** aubergine dip made from baked aubergines, liquidised with tomatoes, onions and lemon juice

**Moussaka** moussaka, made from fried slices of aubergines, interlayered with minced lamb or beef and béchamel sauce

**Pastítsio** layers of macaroni, haloumi cheese and minced meat (cooked with onions, tomatoes and basil), topped with béchamel sauce and baked

**Píta me kymá** meat pie made from minced lamb and eggs, flavoured with onions and cinnamon and baked in filo pastry

**Saláta horiátiki** country salad (known in Britain as 'Greek salad'); every restaurant has its own recipe for this salad, but the basic ingredients comprise tomatoes, cucumber, onions, green peppers, black olives, oregano and feta cheese dressed with vinegar, olive oil and even more oregano

**Souvlaki** kebab – usually of pork, cooked over charcoal

**Spanakotyropitákia** cigar-shaped pies made from feta cheese, eggs, spinach, onions and nutmeg in filo pastry

**Taramasalata** dip made from puréed potatoes, smoked cod's roe, oil, lemon juice and onion

**Tiropitákia** small, triangular cheese pies made from feta cheese and eggs in filo pastry

**Tzatziki** grated cucumber and garlic in a dressing of yoghurt, olive oil and vinegar

◒ Fresh fish is often on the menu

# Shopping

You could easily wear out a pair of flip-flops while shopping in Crete's towns and resorts – the variety of products is wide and if you look and compare carefully you'll find good-quality items at reasonable prices. Shop owners are usually helpful and most speak English. For specialist crafts and local produce, head for the country villages.

## CARPETS & RUGS

Basic woven mats and rugs can be found everywhere at reasonable prices. Better-quality carpets are also available, but be sure to check their authenticity.

⬥ *A colourful array of Cretan delicacies*

## DELICATESSEN CHOICES

The pungent smell of herbs and spices usually announces an Aladdin's cave of local gourmet delights. Honey and intriguing jams such as fig, tangerine and carrot with honey, jars of fruit preserved in sugar syrup, *raki*, even sponge cakes, all jostle for shelf space.

## JEWELLERY

Gold and silver jewellery shops abound with an extensive range of designs. The quality of the jewellery is generally excellent and most gold items are 14 carat. Silver jewellery is particularly good value. Prices of jewellery are unlikely to be displayed, as vendors are not keen on potential rivals undercutting their special rates. Despite this, prices tend to be similar.

## LACE & EMBROIDERY

The choices here are limitless, with bedspreads, tablecloths, mats and clothing available in traditional designs and colours. Displays are particularly enticing in country villages, where the women sit outside working at their craft.

## LEATHER & POTTERY

Leather is one of the island's specialities. Leather Alley, in Chania, has a huge choice of belts, handbags, sandals, satchels and Cretan-style boots but there are many other leather outlets around the island. A wide range of Cretan pottery is available, from basic traditional wine and oil jars to more sophisticated designs and finishes.

## MUSEUM REPLICAS

Many replicas of items on display in Greek museums are on sale in tourist shops, but most are cheap and crude. It is worth paying extra for the excellent reproductions available from recognised museum shops, such as the Loggia, at Rethymnon, and the shops to be found close to the Archaeological Museum entrance in Iraklion.

# Children

Greeks adore children, so having them around presents little problem. The danger is that you will actually be ignored in favour of them. In summer especially, Greek families tend to stay up until after midnight. They congregate in the local square, which is usually closed to traffic after 18.00, for a meal or drink at around 22.00. This makes it safe for children to run around with their friends, while parents relax.

## BOAT TRIPS
Children love being on the water, so play pirates for a day by sailing to a remote beach with a picnic, either on an organised trip or by hiring your own boat. Sailing trips can also include some sightseeing, watching fish through a glass-bottom boat, searching for dolphins or fishing. Trips can be booked from the boat operators at resort harbours, or via your hotel or holiday representative.

## CASTLES & RUINS
For ancient sites and castles with reasonably unrestricted access, try the Minoan palace at Malia, Frangokastelo Castle, Rethymnon Fortress, Pyrgos Castle on Santorini and the fort at Iraklion. Keep a close eye on your children, however, as not all dangerous areas are fenced off or protected.

## WATER PARKS
Try one of several water parks on Crete to make children's dreams come true – they'll be overjoyed at the wide range of fun activities in and around the water for all ages, and parents get a break too as there are plenty of lifeguards around. Expect big slides, whirlpools, black holes, rivers for floating down on tubes and children's playgrounds.
For teenagers, parties are sometimes put on and there are also restaurants, bars and snack bars. Some parks have free admission, charging separately for sunbeds and rides, while others have unlimited access to rides after paying the admission fee.

**Star Beach Water Park** in Hersonissos (see page 55) is located along the beach and additionally offers watersports. ❶ 28970 29351 Ⓦ www.starbeach.gr ⏱ 09.00–19.00

**Water City**, just inland from Kokkini Hani, is Crete's biggest water park (see page 48). ❶ 28107 81317 Ⓦ www.watercity.gr ⏱ 10.00–18.30

## WATERSPORTS

In the main tourist areas there is no shortage of watersports activities for children, such as pedalos and canoes. A flag system is in operation on most beaches, and there is usually a lifeguard on duty.

⏺ *Water parks are great for child-friendly fun*

# Sports & activities

### GO-KARTING
**Hersonissos Kartland** Next to Star Beach Water Park (see page 55)
 28970 25090

### GUIDED WALKS
**The Happy Walker** Rethymnon ❶ 28310 52920 Ⓦ www.happywalker.com
**Trekking Plan** Aghia Marina/Platanias ❶ 28210 60861 Ⓦ www.cycling.gr

### HORSE RIDING
**Melanouri Horse Farm** Lessons for both beginners and the more
advanced. From moonlight rides to trekking through picturesque
olive groves and forgotten villages. Food is provided. ⓐ Near Matala
❶ 28920 45040 Ⓦ www.melanouri.com
**Odysseia Stables** Lessons and guided tours in the pretty villages and
hills overlooking the coast. ⓐ Avdou village, near Hersonissos
❶ 28970 51080 Ⓦ www.horseriding.gr

### MOUNTAIN BIKING
**Paleochora** Notos Car & Motorbike Rental ⓐ Venizelos ❶ 28230 42110
Ⓦ www.notoscar.com
**Santorini** Motor Inn ⓐ Kamari ❶ 22860 31165 Ⓦ www.motorinn.gr

### SAILING
**Chania** Venetian harbour, *Evangelos* glass-bottom boat.
**Hersonissos** MS *Calypso*, Dia Island, snorkelling, barbecue.
**Rethymnon** Venetian harbour, Dolphin Cruises (❶ 28310 57666
Ⓦ www.dolphin-cruises.com), Albatross fishing trips and the Captain
Hook Pirate Ship.

### SCUBA DIVING
**Anissaras (Hersonissos)** Coral Diving Center ⓐ Poseidon ❶ 28970 23282
Ⓦ www.coraldiving.gr

**Gouves** Big Blue Diving School 🅐 Aphrodite Hotel, Beach road
🕾 28970 42363
**Rethymnon** Paradise Diving Center 🅐 West of Rethymnon at Petres
🕾 28310 26317 🅦 www.diving-center.gr

## TENNIS
**Chania** Tennis Club 🅐 Near the airport 🕾 28210 24010

## WATERSPORTS CENTRES
There is a whole range of watersports activities available all along the
island's coastline. Below are just a few places to try.
**Chania** A whole range available from operators along the shore
between Platanias and Chania.
**Hersonissos** A wide range of watersports on the main beach.
**Kokkini Hani** Club Papillon on Thermis beach offers a good range of
watersports.
**Rethymnon** Watersports available on the main town beach, including
speedboat hire and fishing.
**Stalis** Opportunities for skyride, paragliding and watersports; Sea Wolf
Watersports also offers a full range of activities, or try Zervas, in front of
Zervas Hotel.

🔺 *Jet-skis offer fun for all*

● A traditional Cretan dancer

# Festivals & events

*Panigiria* (religious festivals) play a large part in Greek culture, especially saints' days. Wine festivals are held around the island in the autumn. Additionally, most towns and large resorts organise cultural festivals between late June and early September featuring classical or pop concerts, theatre, culinary events and special exhibitions. Check out dates and venues at the local tourist office. The most important public holiday is Ochi Day, on 28 October. *Papas* (priests) still play a large part in the life of the community. Although younger Greeks are less inclined to religion, the Papa is still called in to bless a new car, shop and even traffic lights. Organised folk evenings are the nearest most tourists get to Greek folk culture, but some restaurants have live music and maybe some dancing.

## SAINTS' DAYS

The whole of Greece would be on permanent holiday if every saint's day was celebrated but, fortunately, only major saints warrant a near shutdown. Villages often have their own saint, so it is not unusual to arrive unexpectedly in the middle of a celebration, which always starts with a church service, before the real business of feasting and dancing begins. Among the feasts that are celebrated island-wide are the following.

- **23 April**  St George
- **24 June**  John the Baptist
- **20 July**  Profitis Ilias (the Prophet Elijah – to whom most small churches on hilltops are dedicated)
- **15 August**  Assumption of the Virgin – one of the biggest feasts in the Cretan calendar
- **25 August**  Aghios Titos in Iraklion
- **11 November**  St Minas Protector, patron saint of Iraklion

## EASTER

The greatest festival in Greece is Easter, which is more important even than Christmas. Almost everything shuts down for at least three days, and it can be difficult to find a bus or taxi. The date of the Greek Orthodox Easter is movable and only coincides with the rest of Europe every few years.

**Good Friday**  Tolling bells and yellow candles accompany the solemn processions in the evening, parading the flower-decorated bier of the dead Christ.

**Easter Saturday**  Evening service ends as all lights are extinguished at midnight. To the deafening sound of church bells and firecrackers, the priest lights a candle – the flame of which is then used to light the white candles of the congregation with the announcement *Christos anesti* (Christ has arisen).

**Easter Sunday**  Easter is celebrated with spit-roasted lamb and *raki*.

▶ *A pretty scene in Chania*

# PRACTICAL INFORMATION
Tips & advice

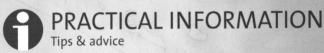

# Accommodation

Crete has thousands of hotels, offering accommodation in all price classes – the following is a brief selection. Price ratings are based on double-room rate with breakfast in high season:

£ under €75  ££ €75–150  £££ over €150

### AGHIA GALINI

**Palazzo Greco Boutique Hotel ££** Sporting great sea views, this boutique hotel has a full range of facilities and is on the main road within easy walking distance of both the beach and the town centre. ❶ 28230 91187 Ⓦ www.palazzogreco.com

### AGHIA MARINA

**Haris Hotel ££** A popular beachside hotel near Aghia Marina's village centre with comfortable rooms. Facilities include a garden, pool, children's play area, organised entertainment, beach chairs and parasols. ⓐ 242 Aghia Marina, main road ❶ 28210 68816 Ⓦ www.hotel-haris.com

### AGHIOS NIKOLAOS

**Kastro Hotel ££** Bright, sunny rooms and apartments with views of the harbour and town centre. ⓐ Odos Lasthenous 23 ❶ 28410 24918

### CHANIA

**Porto del Colombo ££** A 600-year-old building in a maze of narrow alleys, and still sporting a Turkish hammam and a prison room. The ten hotel rooms are comfy, some with great views. ⓐ Odos Theofanous ❶ 28210 98466 Ⓦ www.portodelcolombo.com

**Porto Veneziano Hotel ££** A stylish new Best Western hotel overlooking the harbour and only a few minutes' walk from the sights and the town beach. ⓐ Old Venetian harbour ❶ 28210 27100 Ⓦ www.portoveneziano.gr

## GOUVES

**Astir Beach Hotel ££** A large and pleasant beachside hotel with simple rooms, a good swimming pool and a restaurant. ☏ 28970 41141 Ⓦ www.astirbeach.gr

## HERSONISSOS

**Maragakis Beach Hotel ££** A large central option near the town beach and a short walk from the nightlife options. The hotel has a good pool. ⓐ Beach road ☏ 28970 22405 Ⓦ www.maragakis.gr

## IRAKLION

**Megaron £££** A fantastic five-star hotel dating back to the 1920s and ideally positioned between the harbour and old town. ⓐ Odos Beaufort 9 ☏ 28103 05300 Ⓦ www.gdmmegaron.gr

## MALIA

**Malia Beach Hotel ££–£££** A beautifully landscaped hotel directly on the sandy beach with salt and freshwater swimming pools, tennis courts, mini-golf and other activities. ☏ 28970 31003 Ⓦ www.maliabeach.gr

## PALEOCHORA

**Caravella Apartments ££** A short walk from the centre of town, overlooking the sandy beach. Designer apartments with kitchens and large terraces. ⓐ Odos Voutas ☏ 28230 41131 Ⓦ www.caravella.gr

## RETHYMNON

**Brascos Hotel £** Next to the city garden, this mid-range hotel has great views from the rooftop garden and makes a convenient base. ⓐ Moatsou and Daskalaki 1 ☏ 28310 23721 Ⓦ www.brascos.com

## STALIS

**Zephiros Beach Hotel ££** Stylish air-conditioned rooms in a hotel with large pool, right on Stalis' sandy beach. ⓐ Aghios Ioannis ☏ 28970 31566 Ⓦ www.zephiros.gr

# Preparing to go

## GETTING THERE

The cheapest way to get to Crete is to book a package holiday with one of the leading tour operators. Those specialising in Crete offer flight-only deals or combined flight-and-accommodation packages at prices that are hard to beat by booking direct. If your travelling times are flexible, and if you can avoid the school holidays, you can also find excellent last-minute deals on the Internet. Make sure you also check the travel supplements of newspapers such as the *Sunday Telegraph* and the *Sunday Times* for inexpensive flights and privately owned villas and apartments. You can also choose to use one of many budget airlines flying to Greece; see Ⓦ www.whichbudget.com for a complete overview of connections.

### By air

Crete currently has two international airports. Chania serves the west of the island and Heraklion the centre and east. Sitia's airport is currently being upgraded to handle international flights and will soon be a handy option for eastern Crete. There are numerous charter and budget airline companies offering flights to Crete during the summer months, although if you travel out of season, you may have to use a scheduled flight with **Olympic Air** (Ⓣ 30 210 3550500 Ⓦ www.olympicair.com) or **Aegean Airlines** (Ⓣ 30 210 6261000 Ⓦ www.aegeanair.com). If you can be flexible about when you visit, you can pick up relatively inexpensive special deals. As a rule, the further in advance you buy your ticket, the cheaper it usually is – but you can also get good last-minute deals from online travel agents via the Internet.

Many people are aware that air travel emits $CO_2$, which contributes to climate change. You may be interested in the possibility of lessening the environmental impact of your flight through the charity **Climate Care**, which offsets your $CO_2$ by funding environmental projects around the world. Visit Ⓦ www.jpmorganclimatecare.com

## TRAVEL INSURANCE

Although Greece is a very safe country when it comes to petty crime and has a good healthcare system, it's a good idea to purchase travel insurance before you go to Crete as serious accidents may require you to return home. Check the policy carefully regarding medical coverage, dental treatment, loss of baggage, flight cancellations, repatriation and so on, and whether activities like scuba diving, horse riding and watersports need extra coverage. Keep all medical receipts for claim purposes; if your possessions are stolen, you'll also need to file a police report.

UK visitors carrying a European Health Insurance Card (EHIC) get reduced-cost and sometimes free state-provided medical treatment in Greece and most other European countries. The free card can be ordered via the **Department of Health** (☎ 0845 606 2030 ⓦ www.dh.gov.uk) or pick up an EHIC form from the post office.

## TOURIST INFORMATION

In the UK, the **Greek National Tourist Office** (ⓐ 4 Conduit Street, London W1S 2DJ ☎ 020 7495 9300 ⓦ www.gnto.co.uk ⓔ info@gnto.co.uk) can provide general information about visiting Greece, and has useful brochures and maps that you can download online or order.

## BEFORE YOU LEAVE

Avoid last-minute panics and stress by making your preparations well in advance. It is not necessary to have inoculations to travel in Europe, but you should make sure you and your family are up to date with the basics, such as tetanus. It is a good idea to pack a small first-aid kit to carry with you containing plasters, antiseptic cream, travel sickness pills, insect repellent and/or bite-relief cream, antihistamine tablets, upset stomach remedies and painkillers. Suntan lotion and after-sun cream are often more expensive in Crete than in the UK so it is worth taking a good selection – especially of the higher-factor lotions for children.

If you are taking prescription medicines, ensure that you have enough for the duration of your visit – you may find it impossible to obtain the same medicines in Crete.

## ENTRY FORMALITIES

All EU and other citizens from all Western countries only need a passport to enter Greece. Visas are only required by certain nationalities; details can be found on the **Greek Foreign Ministry** website Ⓦ www.mfa.gr. Check well in advance that your passport is up to date and has at least three months left to run after your return (six months is even better). All children, including newborn babies, need their own passports. It generally takes at least three weeks to process a passport renewal, and often even longer in the run-up to the summer months, so don't leave it to the last minute to organise. For the latest information on how to renew your passport and the processing times, contact the **Identity & Passport Service** (Ⓣ 0300 222 0000 Ⓦ www.passport.gov.uk). Check the details of your travel tickets well before your departure, ensuring that the timings and dates are correct. If you plan to rent a car while on Crete, be sure to have your driving licence (and that of any other drivers) with you; carrying an international driving licence is not necessary.

## MONEY

Like many EU countries, Greece uses the euro. Euro (€) note denominations are 500, 200, 100, 50, 20, 10 and 5. Coins are 1 and 2 euros and 1, 2, 5, 10, 20 and 50 centimos (also called lepta). The best way to get euros in Greece is by using your debit bank card in ATMs, which can be found in all towns, resorts and airports. Make sure you know your PIN and check with your bank to see if there are any charges for using your card abroad. Credit cards are increasingly accepted in hotels and restaurants across Crete but less so in shops and supermarkets. Make sure that your credit and debit cards are up to date and that your credit limit is sufficient to allow you to make those holiday purchases.

You can purchase cash euros before leaving the UK, but keep in mind that changing cash locally at a bank or exchange office will be much better value. Euro-denomination traveller's cheques, which can be purchased at UK exchange offices and banks, are a safe way to carry money as you'll be refunded if the cheques are lost or stolen, but they're used less and less in Europe and can be a hassle to change.

## CLIMATE

Average daytime temperatures: April 20°C (68°F); May 24°C (75°F); June 27°C (81°F); July 29°C (84°F); August 28°C (82°F); September 26°C (79°F); October 23°C (73°F).

You will often find that the southern coast experiences temperatures up to 10°C (18°F) higher. In spring and autumn you might need a sweater at night, especially if you want to eat outside. Crete has quite high humidity, more so in the west, which often makes it feel hotter than it is. The best dress rule to follow is to wear layers so that if you get too hot, you only need to remove a shirt or sweater.

## BAGGAGE ALLOWANCE

Baggage allowances vary according to the airline, destination and the class of travel, but 20 kg (44 lb) per person is the norm for luggage that is carried in the hold; check your ticket to see if the weight limit is mentioned there. Large items – surfboards, golf clubs, collapsible wheelchairs and pushchairs – are usually charged as extras, and it is a good idea to let the airline know in advance if you want to bring these. You are allowed only one item of hand baggage (check measurements with your airline) plus any airport purchases, umbrella, handbag, coat, camera, etc. Note that security measures at both UK and Greek airports prohibit you from taking any sharp objects or any liquids and gels in your hand baggage, unless necessary for the flight and packed in containers no larger than 100 ml (3.5 fl oz) inside a resealable plastic bag. Read more about the security rules on your departure airport website.

# During your stay

### AIRPORTS

Both airports on Crete are served by good roads. Iraklion airport is connected to the city centre by city buses running several times an hour (purchase your ticket from the kiosk beside the bus stop), while Chania airport only has limited numbers of public buses running to town every day (schedule posted outside the building; tickets from the driver). Taxis are readily available at both airports, and all rental-car agencies have offices at the airports. Note that it's often cheaper to arrange car hire in advance, and that in high season cars can be difficult to come by without advance booking.

### COMMUNICATIONS

The Greek national phone company, OTE, has public phones in all towns, villages and resorts which accept OTE phonecards and have English-language instructions. Some resorts have private coin-operated phone booths but these are usually very bad value. You can also make calls from many kiosks or from *kafeneion* in smaller villages; they have a metering system and you will be told how much your call costs at the end. Using a €5 prepaid calling card (available at any kiosk) is the cheapest way to phone abroad. These can be used from any OTE public phone or hotel phone (dial a free local number, then follow the English-language instructions to enter your code and call the number you wish to reach).

Many tourists bring their mobile phones and use roaming to phone home. Check the charges carefully as this can be a very expensive way to phone home. If you're planning to phone often and want to be reached as well, consider buying a local Cosmote or Vodafone SIM card (available from many kiosks and mobile-phone shops for a few euros) so you have a local number, incurring lower costs.

Most post offices are open Monday to Friday 07.30–14.00, the main ones in Chania and Iraklion until 19.30 and on Saturdays. During the tourist season there are also mobile post offices – big yellow caravans, which appear in several tourist areas. They are often open on Saturdays and Sundays. Postboxes are bright yellow with a blue logo; at major post offices you will find two slots: *esoterik* for local mail and *exoterik* for overseas. Outside the main towns they are not always emptied every day. Postcards can take up to two weeks to get to Britain, letters three or four days; if you want your postcards to arrive back home before you do then put them in an envelope. Sending a postcard or letter abroad costs €0.62.

## TELEPHONING GREECE
All telephone numbers in Greece, whether landline or mobile phones, consist of ten digits, and there are no additional city codes. To make a call within Greece, simply dial these ten digits. To call to Greece from abroad or from your mobile phone while in the country, dial the international access code, usually 00, followed by Greece's country code 30 and the ten-digit local number.

## TELEPHONING ABROAD
To call abroad from Greece, dial 00 followed by the country code (44 for the UK, 353 for Ireland, 1 for the US, 61 for Australia, 64 for New Zealand and 27 for South Africa) followed by the city code (minus the initial 0) and the subscriber's number.

## CUSTOMS
Cretans are renowned for their *filoxenia* (hospitality to strangers) and you are bound to experience it in one way or another during your stay. If you are invited to eat or drink with a Cretan it is considered insulting if you try to pay your share; you can always try to reciprocate with a gift at a later time (a bottle of whisky is considered a good present), but be warned: if you make a gift they will try to give you something in return! Especially in the hotter summer months, most Cretans take a siesta between 14.00 and 17.00, one of the reasons why a lot of shops are closed during that time. Cretans rarely begin their evening meal earlier

than 21.00, and usually take the whole family along, babies too. Children are generally allowed to wander around restaurants at will, even late at night. When drinking in the company of a Cretan, never fill their glass to the top – it is considered to be an insult.

## DRESS CODES

If you are visiting churches or monasteries, you will not be allowed in wearing shorts or beach clothes; it is best to wear long trousers or a skirt and take a shirt or wrap to cover your shoulders. Some churches provide clothing for visitors to dress up in. If you are invited into a private home in Crete, again it is impolite to arrive in shorts – Cretans love to dress up, whether to go out or to entertain at home. Topless or nude sunbathing is officially forbidden but still common in beach resorts; judge the situation before stripping and causing upset.

## ELECTRICITY

Voltage in Crete is 220 volts, which is compatible with the UK, but you will need a two-pin adaptor to fit Greek sockets. It is important to realise that electricity is expensive in Greece, so be considerate in your use of it; for example, do not leave air conditioning on in your room when you go out. There may be power cuts due to excessive demands, but these rarely last long. If you are buying electrical appliances to take home, always check that they will work in the UK before you buy.

## EMERGENCIES

The general emergency number for ambulance, police and fire brigade is 112.

The best medical care on Crete is found in Iraklion; try the private **Creta InterClinic** (ⓐ Odos Minoas 63, Iraklion ⓣ 28103 73800 ⓦ www.cic.gr ⓔ info@cretainterclinic.gr) or the **Venizelio Hospital** (ⓐ Leoforos Knossos, Iraklion ⓣ 28103 68000).
**British Vice Consulate**: ⓐ Candia Tower, Odos Thalita 17, Plateia Agios Dimitrios, Iraklion ⓣ 28102 24012 ⓦ http://ukingreece.fco.gov.uk ⓔ crete@fco.gov.uk

## GETTING AROUND

### Driving conditions

Remember that in Crete you drive on the right. Always carry with you your driving licence, passport and any other relevant documents when driving. Get a good road map (often provided by the rental company), as signposting is quite bad. Despite 4,000 years of civilisation, even a major site like Knossos is not properly signposted from nearby Iraklion. Be prepared to do many U-turns! The confusing Greek signposting philosophy is to indicate smaller destinations off the main road and not to continue to confirm the town you're heading to – be sure to bear this in mind if it's unclear which is the main and which the side road.

Road quality on Crete is generally quite good, with only smaller roads and unsurfaced tracks requiring you to slow down to protect your wheel rims. The national highway is a good wide road that runs across the top of the island linking the four main cities all the way from Kastelli to Malia; unfortunately, Greek-style signposting means it can be tricky to find a way to get on it! On roads like the national highway, what would appear to be the hard shoulder is in fact the slow lane, used to allow faster traffic to pass. In high season roads get very busy so beware of slow drivers, holidaymakers on quad motorbikes, farmers watering their olives, and traffic jams.

If you are stopped by the police for a motoring offence, you are expected to pay your fine on the spot (make sure you get a receipt if you do). If you do not pay, the police will remove the licence plates from your car, which you will then have to reclaim from the police station on payment of the fine. If anything like this happens, you should contact your hire company immediately.

### Car hire & driving

Drivers need to be over 21 (25 in some cases) and have a valid driving licence. Car hire is available at all resorts and costs €30–60 per day for a small car, depending on season and length of rental. Local rental companies in the beach resorts often have lower prices than the international companies in the main towns. Most rental cars are new

and zippy small cars, and air conditioning is quite common. Open-top 4WDs are popular too but much pricier. Insurance is included in your car rental, but is sometimes not valid if you use non-asphalted roads, and check that it includes damage to the wheels, tyres and roof.

### Public transport
Crete's bus service is quite good and cheap. All buses are new, air-conditioned coaches and usually run on time. In cities, printed timetables can be found at the bus station, where you can also buy tickets in advance. When getting on in villages and resorts you usually pay the conductor after getting seated. Buses run regularly between major towns, particularly along the north coast. **KTEL**, the national bus company, regards its timetables as a state secret, and online timetables can only be found for western Crete (Ⓦ www.bus-service-crete-ktel.com).

### Taxis
Taxis can be found at arrival points, major hotels and driving around larger resorts. They're comparatively inexpensive to use, and prices for longer distances are usually fixed.

## HEALTH, SAFETY & CRIME
### Healthcare
There are a number of private medical clinics offering a 24-hour service and with English-speaking doctors. Details are available at local pharmacies or the small 'health houses' found in most resorts.

Pharmacies often have English-speaking staff and are very helpful for minor complaints and illnesses. They operate a rota system for opening outside normal shop hours (especially at the weekend) and information about the duty chemist is displayed in each shop. Generally, both over-the-counter and prescription drugs purchased at pharmacies in Crete will be cheaper than in England. However, some, such as antibiotics, can be expensive. Homeopathic and herbal treatments and remedies are very popular in Crete and widely available. Personal hygiene goods are to be found in most supermarkets.

## Food & water

Travellers who are not used to olive oil may experience minor stomach problems for a few days – olive oil is good for your health so it's worth getting used to it! Tap water is safe enough, but bottled water is widely available, cheap and tastes much better.

## Precautions

Cooling breezes off the sea can mask the intensity of the sun's rays, which can burn you if reflected off sand or nearby water. You can even burn in the shade, especially if you have sensitive skin. If you drive a car with an open sun roof, keep your shoulders covered and wear a hat. The same applies if you are wandering around shopping. Keep covered up during the hottest part of the day and drink plenty of water to avoid dehydration.

Sea urchins are quite common in rocky coastal regions; if you step on one the spines can be removed with tweezers. You should then douse the affected area with lemon juice or ammonia; you can buy ammonia 'sticks', which are also good for jellyfish stings, at pharmacies.

Mosquitoes can be a nuisance but are easily dealt with by burning insect coils or using an electric deterrent.

## Safety & crime

Compared to most Western European countries, Greece is a very safe place, with hardly any petty or violent crime – in fact, it's mainly other tourists, and not Greeks, that you have to be wary of! A forgotten camera or wallet will most likely still be on the restaurant table when you return for it, and public drunkenness or violence is quite rare. Still, avoid temptation by leaving all valuables and documents in the hotel safe and carrying only what you need. Be wary for bag snatchers in busy resorts and towns, and leave your car empty when you park it. The civil police keep a low profile but invariably turn up when needed, at motor accidents and crime scenes, and to deal with illegally parked cars. Parking in the narrow streets of towns and villages can be a problem. The police may show tolerance towards local inhabitants over parking, but are less inclined to treat hire cars with the same degree of leniency. There are also tourist police, who speak several languages and are trained to help with problems faced by tourists.

### Restricted areas & photography

Greece has very strict rules about photographing any military installation, and there are many army, navy and air force bases that are surrounded with signs telling you not to take pictures. Civilian airports are often also used by the military, and taking photos there is forbidden too. It is worth remembering that the 2001 case of British plane spotters in mainland Greece being tried for and convicted of spying was based not on photographs taken, but on information they wrote down in notebooks.

### MEDIA

Even the smaller resorts sell English newspapers, usually only a day or two out of date. Locally produced newspapers in English can be a useful source of information about local events.

### OPENING HOURS

Shops traditionally open 08.00–13.30 on Monday and Wednesday, 08.00–13.30 and 17.30–20.30 on Tuesday, Thursday and Friday, and 08.00–13.30 on Saturday. Tourist resorts are a case apart and most shops open all day, usually from early morning until 23.00. Sunday is a general closing day, but touristy shops mostly remain open.

Restaurants usually open for lunch and dinner, and close for a few hours in between. Timings can be erratic and will often change according to the day of the week and the season.

Banks are generally open 08.00–14.00 on Monday to Thursday and 08.00–13.30 on Friday.

Churches are almost always open for visiting, but in villages you often have to find the person who looks after the key.

## RELIGION

Crete is dominated by the Greek Orthodox Church with a faith that has strong historical roots in the local community. Saints' days and name days are very important days to celebrate, but their religious overtones are quickly lost to the Cretan enthusiasm for feasting and dancing. The attitude is very much 'work hard and play hard', but the church and religion are still a very big part of everyday life, especially in the villages. Weddings, baptisms and funerals are serious and lengthy occasions.

## TIME DIFFERENCES

Crete is in the same time zone as eastern Europe, therefore 2 hours ahead of the UK. Clocks go forward 1 hour on the last Sunday in March and back 1 hour on the last Sunday in October, just as in Britain.

## TIPPING

In restaurants a service or cover charge is often included in your bill. However, it is accepted that a small tip will be given to the waiters – usually you will find your change contains several coins which (within reason, and only if you feel inclined to) you leave behind. It is also customary to tip taxi drivers, hotel porters, chambermaids and hairdressers. If you are shown around a church by the 'keyholder' or priest, a tip is also welcome, but this should always be left in the donations box rather than offered directly to the guide.

## TOILETS

Public toilets are found in bus stations and main squares. Smarter facilities are found in bars, but you should buy a drink or ask nicely if you want to use them. Toilets are generally very clean, but you must observe the practice throughout Greece and not flush away used toilet paper. Do as the Greeks do and put it in a bin (provided in each cubicle) next to the toilet. Remember this, or you risk blocking the pipes!

## TRAVELLERS WITH DISABILITIES

Both international airports and the newer top-class hotels have special toilets, but sadly that appears to be the extent to which Crete accommodates the disabled. Overall, the island is distinctly short of amenities for visitors with disabilities. Organisations for the disabled at home can advise on suitable hotels and resorts and may be able to put you in touch with somebody who has first-hand experience of holidaying in Crete. In general, however, you will find Cretans are considerate and helpful towards those with disabilities.

## A

accommodation 110–11
Afrata 24
Aghia Galini 32–5, 110
Aghia Marina 22–5, 110
Aghia Roumeli 71, 73
Aghia Triada 76
Aghios Georgios 82
Aghios Nikolaos 11, 65–8, 110
air travel 112, 116
Akrotiri 86–7
Almyros 65
Anissaras 52
aquarium 50
archaeological sites 10, 48, 63, 74–80, 86–7
Argyropouli 30
Arkadi Monastery 30
ATMs 114

## B

baggage allowance 115
banks 122
beaches see individual locations
boat trips 16, 20, 28, 33–4, 54, 61, 63, 67, 85–6, 87, 102
buses 120

## C

car hire 114, 119–20
caves 37–8, 81–2
Chania 10, 11, 14–19, 105, 110
children 102–3
climate 115
credit and debit cards 114
Cretaquarium 50
crime 121–2
currency 114
customs, local 117–18
cycling 23

## D

Diktean Cave 81–2
disabilities, travellers with 124
diving 11, 16, 28, 50, 52, 90, 104–5

dress codes 118
drinking water 121
driving 24, 114, 119–20, 121–2

## E

eating out 94–9
    see also individual locations
El Greco 44, 46
Elafonissi 11, 21
electricity 118
emergencies 118
Episkopi 24

## F

Faistos 10, 74, 76
festivals and events 107–8
Fira (Thira) 88–9
Fodele 44, 46
food and drink 94–9, 101

## G

glass-bottomed boat tours 11, 16, 54, 67
go-karting 18, 54, 104
golf 54, 68
Gortys 74, 75
Gouves 50–51, 111

## H

health 113, 120–21
health hazards 121
Hersónissos 11, 52–6, 105, 111
horse riding 38, 54, 104
hot springs 86, 87

## I

insurance 113
Iraklion 40–47, 111

## K

kafeneion (café) 97
Kamari 86, 90
Knossos 10, 77–80
Kokkini Hani 48–9, 105
Kolymbari 24

Koutouloufari 54
Kritsa 9, 68

**L**
language 98–9
Lasithi Plateau 10, 81–2
Lefka Ori 8
Lissos 21
Lychnostatis Open-Air Museum 57–8

**M**
Malia 11, 61–4, 111
Malia Palace 63
Matala 11, 36–9
medical treatment 113, 118, 120
menu decoder 98–9
Mili 30
Mochos 9
money 114–15
Mount Ida 8
mountain biking 90, 104

**N**
newspapers 122

**O**
Oia 83, 86, 91–2
opening hours 122

**P**
Paleochora 20–21, 111
passports and visas 114
Paximadia Island 33–4
pharmacies 120
photography 122
Piskopiano 54
Pitsidia 39
Platanes 27
Platanias 22–5
police 121, 122
post offices 116–17
public transport 120
Pyrgos 86, 87

**R**
religion 123
Rethymnon 10, 26–31, 105, 111

**S**
safety 120–21
sailing 104
Samaria Gorge 8, 10, 70–73
Santorini 10, 83–92
shopping 100–101, 122
    see also individual locations
siesta 117
Sougia 21
Spinalonga 67
sports and activities 104–5
Stalis (Stalida) 57–60, 105, 111
sun safety 72, 73, 121

**T**
taxis 120
telephones 116, 117
tennis 105
time differences 123
tipping 123
toilets 123
tourist information 113
tourist trains 11, 23, 29, 50, 55
traveller's cheques 114–15
trekking 23, 30, 71–3
turtles 31
Tzermiado 82

**V**
volcano 86, 87

**W**
walks, guided 30, 104
water parks 18, 48, 53–4, 55, 102–3
watersports 48, 50, 52, 58, 63, 90, 103, 104–5
White Mountains 8
windmills 81, 82
wine, beer and spirits 87, 96–7
winery tours 87–8

## ACKNOWLEDGEMENTS

We would like to thank all the photographers, picture libraries and organisations for the loan of the photographs reproduced in this book, to whom copyright in the photograph belongs: Alamy, page 106 (John Martin); Dreamstime.com, page 29 (Paul Cowan), page 45 (Fer737ng), page 70 (Trykster), page 85 (Jirsak); Caroline Jones, page 80; Shutterstock, page 103 (bocky); Thomas Cook Tour Operations Ltd, pages 5, 9, 13, 17, 19, 22, 32, 38, 49, 59, 69, 79, 93, 95, 100, 105; Jeroen van Marle, pages 35, 36, 42, 51, 53, 60, 64, 75, 76, 88, 91, 99, 109; World Pictures/Photoshot, pages 10–11.

Project editor: Kate Taylor
Layout: Trevor Double
Proofreaders: Karolin Thomas & Cath Senker
Indexer: Marie Lorimer

### Send your thoughts to
# books@thomascook.com

- Found a beach bar, peaceful stretch of sand or must-see sight that we don't feature?

- Like to tip us off about any information that needs a little updating?

- Want to tell us what you love about this handy, little guidebook and, more importantly, how we can make it even handier?

Then here's your chance to tell all! Send us ideas, discoveries and recommendations today and then look out for your valuable input in the next edition of this title.

Email to the above address or write to:
pocket guides Series Editor, Thomas Cook Publishing, PO Box 227, Unit 9, Coningsby Road, Peterborough PE3 8SB, UK.

# Useful phrases

| English | Greek | Approx pronunciation |
|---------|-------|----------------------|

## BASICS

| English | Greek | Approx pronunciation |
|---------|-------|----------------------|
| Yes | Ναι | *Ne* |
| No | Οχι | *O-khee* |
| Please | Παρακαλώ | *Pa-ra-ka-lh* |
| Thank you | Ευχαριστώ | *Ef-ha-ri-sto* |
| Hello | Γεια σας | *Ya sas* |
| Goodbye | Αντίο | *Andeeo* |
| Excuse me | Με συγχωρείτε | *Me si-nho-ri-te* |
| Sorry | Συγγνώμη | *Sig-no-mi* |
| That's okay | Εντάξει | *En-ta-xi* |
| I don't speak Greek | Δεν μιλώ Ελληνικά | *Den Mi-lo (E-li-ni-ka)* |
| Do you speak English? | Μιλάτε Αγγλικά; | *Mi-la-te an-gli-ka?* |
| Good morning | Καλημέρα | *Ka-li-me-ra* |
| Good afternoon | χαίρετε | *He-re-te* |
| Good evening | Καλησπέρα | *Ka-li-spe-ra* |
| Goodnight | Καληνύχτα | *Ka-li-nih-ta* |
| My name is ... | Ονομάζομαι | *O-no-ma-zo-me* |

## NUMBERS

| English | Greek | Approx pronunciation |
|---------|-------|----------------------|
| One | Ένα | *E-na* |
| Two | Δύο | *Di-o* |
| Three | Τρία | *Tri-a* |
| Four | Τέσσερα | *Te-se-ra* |
| Five | Πέντε | *Pen-te* |
| Six | Έξι | *E-xi* |
| Seven | Επτά | *Ep-ta* |
| Eight | Οκτώ | *Ok-to* |
| Nine | Εννέα | *E-ne-a* |
| Ten | Δέκα | *De-ka* |
| Twenty | Είκοσι | *I-ko-si* |
| Fifty | Πενήντα | *Pe-nin-ta* |
| One hundred | Εκατό | *E-ka-to* |

## SIGNS & NOTICES

| English | Greek | Approx pronunciation |
|---------|-------|----------------------|
| Airport | Αεροδρόμιο | *A-e-rodromio* |
| Railway station | Σιδηροδρομικός εταμςς | *Sidirodromikos Stathmos* |
| Smoking/ non-smoking | Για Καπνιστές/ Για μη καπνιστές | *Ya kapnistes/ Ya mikapnistes* |
| Toilets | Τουαλέτα | *tualeta* |
| Ladies/Gentlemen | Γυναικών/Ανδρών | *Yinekon/Andron* |